## Access to A-Level H

General Editor: Keith Randell

# France: The Third Republic, 1870–1914

Keith Randell

## Edward Arnold

A division of Hodder & Stoughton

LONDON   MELBOURNE   AUCKLAND

First published in Great Britain 1986
Third impression 1989

British Library Cataloguing in Publication Data

Randell, Keith
  France: The Third Republic, 1870–1914.
  – (Access to A-Level History)
  1. France – History – Third Republic,
  1870–1940
  I. Title    II. Series
  944.081     DC335

  ISBN 0-7131-7481-1

Printed in Great Britain for Edward Arnold, the educational,
academic and medical publishing division of Hodder and Stoughton
Limited, Mill Road, Dunton Green, Sevenoaks, Kent by
St Edmundsbury Press Limited, Bury St Edmunds, Suffolk.

# Contents

# Preface

## To the teacher

The *Access to A-Level History* series has been planned with the A-level student specifically in mind. The text of each volume has been made sufficiently expansive to allow the reader to complete a section without needing to re-read paragraphs in order to 'unpack' condensed narrative or to 'tease out' obscure meanings. The amount of factual detail is suitable for the requirements of A-level, and care has been taken to ensure that all the 'facts' included have been explained or placed in context so as to allow proper understanding. Differing interpretations of events are discussed as appropriate and extracts from sources are woven into the main text. This is essential if A-level students are to be encouraged to argue a case, bringing in suitable evidence to substantiate their points. The hope is that the text will be sufficiently interesting to increase student motivation towards reading history books, and sufficiently stimulating to encourage students to think analytically about what they have learnt.

It is also intended that the series will offer direct assistance to students in preparing to answer both essay and source-based questions. It is expected that the help with source-based questions will be particularly welcomed. The sections providing guidance to the student which appear at the end of each chapter could be used either as a basis for class discussion or by students when working on their own. Direct help is also given with note making and realistic suggestions are made for further reading.

## To the student

Many of you will find that this suggested procedure will enable you to derive the most benefit from each book:

1   Read a whole chapter as fast as you can, and preferably in one sitting.
2   Study the flow diagram at the end of the chapter, ensuring that you understand the general pattern of events covered.
3   Study the 'Answering essay questions on . . .' section at the end of the chapter, consciously identifying the major issues involved.
4   Read the 'Making notes on . . .' section at the end of the chapter, and decide on the pattern of notes you will make.
5   Read the chapter a second time, stopping at each * or chapter sub-heading to make notes on what you have just read.
6   Attempt the 'Source-based questions on . . .' section at the end of the chapter.

When you have finished the book decide whether you need to do further reading on the topic. This will be important if you are seriously aspiring to a high grade at A-level. The 'Further Reading' section at the end of the book will help you decide what to choose.

I wish you well with your A-level studies. I hope they are both enjoyable and successful. If you can think of any ways in which this book could be more useful to students please write to me with your suggestions.

Keith Randell

CHAPTER 1

# Introduction, France: The Third Republic, 1870–1914

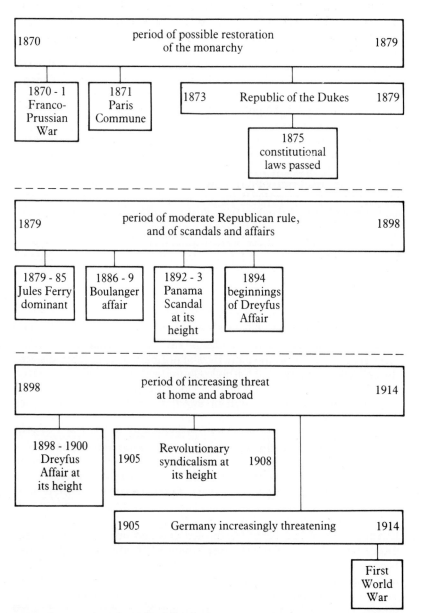

| 1870 | period of possible restoration of the monarchy | 1879 |

| 1870 - 1 Franco-Prussian War | 1871 Paris Commune | 1873 Republic of the Dukes 1879 |

| 1875 constitutional laws passed |

| 1879 | period of moderate Republican rule, and of scandals and affairs | 1898 |

| 1879 - 85 Jules Ferry dominant | 1886 - 9 Boulanger affair | 1892 - 3 Panama Scandal at its height | 1894 beginnings of Dreyfus Affair |

| 1898 | period of increasing threat at home and abroad | 1914 |

| 1898 - 1900 Dreyfus Affair at its height | 1905 Revolutionary syndicalism at its height 1908 |

| 1905 Germany increasingly threatening 1914 |

| First World War |

*Summary – France: The Third Republic, 1870–1914*

To observers from abroad the political life of France from 1870 to 1914 must have resembled a strange circus act, a mixture of tight-rope walking and clowns' routines. Governments appeared to fall and be replaced with monotonous regularity and political scandal was always in the air. In Britain in particular, a widespread smug complacency existed at the way 'progress' in domestic politics was being made in a controlled and orderly manner. The French experience was generally viewed as a combination of tragedy and farce, which merely confirmed the basic lack of good sense and reliability of foreigners. Even now, when more than a century has elapsed since many of the events took place, there is a temptation to regard the politics of the Third Republic as a joke. This temptation is to be resisted.

The French way of doing things was very different from that of the British, Americans and Germans. But then they had a very different situation with which to contend. Ever since the Revolution of 1789, political life had been vibrant and contentious, especially among the educated and the town dwellers. Because of the emotional fervour that accompanied most French activities, the spirit of compromise was singularly lacking. It has been said that there were as many political points of view in France as there were Frenchmen. Truthful as this is in focusing attention on the tradition of drawing fine distinctions in French politics, it hides the fact that there were really only two political standpoints to be taken. You were either in favour of the Revolution and what it had stood for or you were against it.

Those who were in favour of the Revolution were usually referred to as the Left. They tended to favour liberty at the expense of authority, and so were generally hostile to the idea of a strong government that could interfere extensively in the daily lives of ordinary people. They disliked the existence of a powerful Catholic Church which attempted to control the way of life of the nation. They defended the right of all people to have an opportunity to become rich or important as a result of their own endeavours, but they resisted the claim of the successful to be given special privileges or to be treated with great deference. The Left was at its strongest in Paris and other commercial centres, and in the rural areas of the south. It had momentary victories, especially in the 1790s and in 1848. But although it conducted much of the agitation that resulted in regimes collapsing at regular intervals, it enjoyed few of the fruits of its labour. These were normally snapped up by the Right.

The Right generally looked upon the Revolution as an evil event, when lawful authority had been overthrown and had been replaced by the unregulated desires of the masses, a time when life and property had been at the mercy of the envious poor. They mainly saw politics as an unpleasant necessity, to be endured in order to ensure the maintenance of law and order and the continuation of a social system which depended on each rank or level knowing and accepting its place. They wanted strong government, whether a monarchy, an empire, or a conservative republic. They wished to see a firm alliance between Church and State, and a powerful army that could further the country's aims by force of arms if necessary. Many of its adherents were men of wealth and social position but in some parts of France, especially in the west, support for the Right extended to all levels of society in both town and country.

The Right had been in power almost continuously between 1815 and 1870. Unfortunately for them, however, they were by 1870 divided into competing factions, each championing the cause of one of the regimes that had been previously overthrown. The Legitimists favoured a return to power of the royal House of Bourbon which had provided France with her kings in the seventeenth and eighteenth centuries and between 1814 and 1830. In contrast, Orleanists supported a return to the style of constitutional monarchy that had existed under Louis–Philippe between 1830 and 1848. As a third alternative, the Bonapartists favoured the imperial regime inaugurated by Napoleon I between 1804 and 1814 and continued by his nephew, Napoleon III, from 1852 to 1870. Some members of the Right were even reluctantly prepared to accept a republican form of government as long as it pursued policies of which they approved, but they were in a small minority in 1870.

The deep divisions in French political life mainly dictated the pattern of events up to 1914. The supporters of the Left in Paris took advantage of the capture of the Emperor, Napoleon III, during the Franco–Prussian War in September 1870, to seize power in the capital and declare a new regime, the Third Republic. But once a national general election was held a few months later, supporters of the Right were elected in a large majority, and it seemed only a question of time before the republic would be replaced by a monarchy of some kind. In response to this possibility the Left in Paris declared themselves independent of the new government and attempted to establish a state made up of a number of self-governing local units called Communes. The rebellion was savagely crushed. When the disunity of the Right coincided with a growing acceptance throughout the country of a continuance of the Republic, it seemed as if a stable system had been found. Constitutional laws were passed in 1875 and after the election of 1881 over 80 per cent of the seats in the Chamber of Deputies (the French equivalent of the House of Commons) were filled by supporters of the regime.

Yet the honeymoon period was to be brief. In the 1885 election the Right doubled its number of seats and in the following 15 years the Republic's continued existence was put into question by a number of 'affairs' and scandals which provided tempting opportunities for the Right to stir up trouble. It was only after 1900 that the Third Republic could be said to have been securely established, but by this time it was coming under attack from the extreme Left which was out of sympathy with a system that seemed designed to protect the status quo. Hardly had this challenge been surmounted than it was followed by the even greater crisis of the First World War. Although the Third Republic was to continue until its destruction at the hands of the Germans in 1940, it never managed the long period of settled stability that would have given it an air of permanence.

The seeming instability of the regime was not totally due to the confrontation of the Left with the Right. It was increased by the structure of government that developed under the Constitutional Laws of 1875. The Left was determined that no one man should be allowed to dominate events in case he should be lured down the road of dictatorship. So, although the Republic had a President, he was limited to almost entirely ceremonial duties. There was even a widespread desire among Republican politicians to ensure that nobody of great distinction was elected to the office. The same attitude tended to prevail when it was decided which ministers should be supported. There were a number of strong men in Republican political circles but they rarely found themselves in office. Their colleagues did not wish to be led by someone who would dominate them, and so the individuals who could have helped the Republic present a stable image were in the main prevented from doing so. The Third Republic was therefore able to establish a system of virtual government by the Assembly, in which the ordinary elected representatives, the Deputies and the Senators, collectively decided what would happen, while the ministers were often little more than administrators. Given this situation, it was not surprising that very little substantial legislation was passed. It sometimes took the Assembly almost all its time to agree a budget.

But what seemed most strange to foreigners was the speed with which ministries came and went. Between 1871 and 1914 there were nearly 50, lasting on average less than a year each. Rarely did they stay long enough to see the conclusion of anything they initiated. Resignations were forced on the merest of pretexts and as soon as anybody seemed to be making a real impact (except in times of crisis) he found his support melting away. This was possible because the defeat of a government did not normally lead to a general election as it did in Britain. By the end of the 1870s it was accepted custom for each Chamber of Deputies to be allowed to run its full term of four years, so politicians ran no risk of losing an electoral contest each time they schemed to oust the ministers of the day. What is more, in securing Deputies from the danger of snap elections, the system inhibited the growth of properly organized political parties, because politicians had no incentive to accept the necessary discipline. If one set of ministers fell they could ensure that the next set would follow the same broad policies. And when it came to general elections they could rely on their own local standing to ensure their return to parliament. They did not need the assistance of swarms of party activists. With over 90 per cent of Deputies natives of the constituency they represented, it was very much a case of prominent people being chosen as long as they agreed with the prevailing leftism or rightism of the area.

So the detailed political composition of the Assembly was mainly a matter of chance. As it happened, the largest single grouping in the Chamber of Deputies throughout to period 1876 to 1902 was of conservative-minded Republicans, known as Opportunists until the mid 1890s, and as Progressists from then on. In as much as they were united, they shared a common desire to see the Republic continue and a common caution about social, economic and political reform. They were prepared for change but only when it could be shown to be really necessary, and were therefore content with a way of working that saw little legislation passed.

From 1902 the Radicals took over as the leading parliamentary grouping. They differed from the Progressists in that they were keen to see reforms passed. They wished to see better protection for the interests of the poor and underprivileged, but they were staunch believers in individualism, arguing that people must be encouraged to stand on their own two feet. In this they were opposed by supporters of the extreme left, the Socialists, who had significant representation in parliament from 1893 onwards. The Socialists had abandoned many of the policies of the traditional Left and were hoping to witness the emergence of a strong collectivist state in which the government would take a strong lead in most aspects of life and would ensure that the interests of the working classes were given top priority.

Despite the efforts of the Socialists, the legislative record of the Third Republic remained slight right up to 1914. So the interests of historians have been in more fundamental matters than who was in office and what laws were passed. The questions that have aroused most debate about the history of France between 1870 and 1914 have been, 'Why did the Third Republic last so long?', 'What were the issues and events that endangered it?', and 'What was the truth about the various scandals and affairs that seemed to occur at frighteningly regular intervals?'. It is these questions that the following chapters will be examining.

---

*Making notes on 'Introduction, France: The Third Republic, 1870–1914'*

The aim of the brief introductory chapter is to explain the context in which political life took place in France between the Franco–Prussian and First World Wars, and to lay out the 'political shape' of the period. Many of the points will make much more sense once the rest of the book has been read. It will therefore be worth your while re-reading this chapter once you have finished your work on the rest of the book.

In the meantime it would be sensible to make very brief notes on what you have read. Do this a paragraph at a time. There are only twelve of them in the chapter. For each one note down a collection of phrases (obviously they need not form a grammatical sentence) which sum up the main point being made. Number them from one to twelve. Below is an example of how the beginning of such a set of brief notes might look:

**France: The Third Republic, 1870–1914**
**Introduction**
1. Foreigners viewed the politics of the Third Republic as a joke.
2. Since 1789 France had been divided between those in favour of the Revolution and those against it.
3. Those in favour of the Revolution – the Left – were against strong governments, the Catholic Church and privilege. Stong in Paris. Had rarely held power.

Your completed notes should not total more than 300 words.

---

*Answering essay questions on 'France: The Third Republic, 1870–1914'*

Essay questions that you are likely to be asked on France 1870–1914 fall into two main categories: those covering the whole or a large part of the period, and those concentrating on a particular topic or issue. You must be prepared to answer questions of either type.

In this short section the types of question covering the wide period will be introduced, so that you can have them in mind as you read the rest of the book. A fuller discussion of them will be found on pages 99–100, which you should read when you have completed your study of all six chapters. A discussion of typical questions on particular topics or issues is to be found at the end of each of Chapters 2, 3, 4, 5 and 6.

As you would already expect, the questions covering the period as a whole tend to concentrate on two main issues:

1. What were the threats to the Third Republic?
2. Why did the Third Republic survive these threats?

Typical 'what threats' questions are:

'What obstacles did the Third Republic in France have to overcome in order to survive into the twentieth century?' (London, 1981)
'What constitutional factors and what crises and dissensions threatened the stability of the Third French Republic in the period 1870–1907?' (SUJB, 1979)
'What internal dangers threatened the stability of the Third French Republic before 1895?' (Oxford, 1985)

Notice that this type of question invites you to make a list of the threats or factors involved. As you read the chapters that follow you should be consciously looking for differing threats or factors to add to your list. The same is true of reasons or explanations of why the Third Republic was able to survive the threats.

Typical 'why survive' questions are:

'Why, by 1914, had the Third Republic proved able to survive the difficulties of its earlier years?' (London, 1979)

' "It was unstable, but it endured." How do you explain this apparent contradiction in the Third French Republic?' (WJEC, 1982)
' "The most remarkable characteristic of the Third French Republic was its ability to survive." Discuss this statement in relation to the years 1871–1914' (Scottish, 1980)

# CHAPTER 2

# The Franco–Prussian War and the Paris Commune, 1870–71

## 1 The Franco–Prussian War

On 19 July 1870 France declared war on Prussia. The Franco–Prussian War of 1870–71 had begun. In France the war was viewed as a way of showing the world that she was still the major power in mainland Europe and that Prussia would have to be content with second place, despite the recent victories she had gained under the political leadership of Bismarck. In Prussia the war was seen as an opportunity to inflict a sharp defeat on France and thus to remove the danger of aggression in the future. Bismarck later claimed that he had provoked France into war so that he could use the situation to bring about a unification of Germany under Prussian leadership. But this was a hope that Bismarck did not make public in the summer of 1870, and was not one that was widely shared by his fellow Prussians who saw the war as arising from the bully-boy behaviour of an overmighty neighbour.

Both sides were confident of victory. Only the most cautious of the French doubted that their armies would be in Berlin, the Prussian capital, within a matter of weeks. After all, the French argued, it was well known that France had about 25 per cent more troops than Prussia, and that the French army was a professional army, made up of long-serving career soldiers, whereas the Prussian army mainly comprised conscripts who served for only a few years before returning to a civilian way of life. Could there be any doubt that the professionals would defeat the amateurs? The Prussians, however, saw things very differently. They were sure that they were better equipped than the French, especially in terms of field guns where their breach-loading models could fire more quickly and over a greater range than the traditional muzzle-loading guns used by the French. The Prussians were also sure that their army was more effective than the French because it was better organized, was led by better officers at all levels, and was trained to make the most of every advantage gained, so that small successes were followed up with vigour and were often turned into major victories.

It was not long before the French realized that they would be fighting to defend their own territory, rather than making use of the maps of Germany that had been supplied to all units of the army. It had been expected that France's army of regulars would be ready to fight days or weeks before the Prussian army of conscripts could be fully mobilized. This was not the case. French plans for concentrating their troops on the border with Prussia were ill-thought out and there was much chaos as, for example, troops arrived at one depot and their equipment was sent to another, and blockages developed on roads and railways due to a lack of thought about where the bottlenecks were likely to be and how they could be avoided. In comparison the Prussian mobilization was swift and carefully planned. As a result the French faced armies that were as large and as ready to fight as their own.

When the fighting began the relative equality was quickly turned into Prussian superiority by the tactics employed. Whereas the units of the French army which were not directly involved in a battle tended to hold their positions in readiness to repulse a subsequent attack, the Prussians had issued orders that when a battle developed all troops in the area were to march towards the sound of gun-fire and were to engage the enemy however they could. Thus, although the French matched the number of Prussians in the battle front as a whole, in battle after battle the Prussians managed to bring more troops into effective action. This numerical superiority, linked with artillery that was much more effective, allowed the Prussians to sweep all before them.

Six weeks after the declaration of war France received a crushing blow. On 3 September one of her two main armies was forced to surrender at Sedan; 83 000 men, including the Emperor, Napoleon III, himself and a majority of the leading generals, had found themselves surrounded and outgunned with little option but to surrender or be slaughtered. For so many men to surrender smacked of treachery to the rest of France, but in fact it was the only alternative to a massive and pointless loss of life.

Once the news of the Emperor's surrender reached Paris it took Republicans only a few hours to organize mass demonstrations and to ensure that a Republic was declared. On 4 September, following tradition, the declaration was made from the balcony of the *hôtel de ville*. Also following tradition – as had happened in 1814, 1830 and 1848 – moderate and well-to-do politicians in the capital rallied swiftly to seize power and to frustrate the aspirations of the social revolutionaries. The leading opponents of Napoleon III in the *Corps Législatif* (the French equivalent of the House of Commons at the time) proclaimed a Government of National Defence. This Government was widely accepted throughout France.

* It might have been expected that the overthrow of the Second Empire would lead to a speedy end to the war. The opposite was the case. The followers of Napoleon III were mostly political realists who were quick to spot where their interests lay: they were in favour of peace after the surrender at Sedan. But the Republicans, both moderates and extremists, tended towards idealism. They regarded patriotism as a virtue and were determined that the national enemy should be defeated at any cost. What is more, they were confident that it could be done. The situation in September 1870 was likened to 1792 when revolutionary France had been threatened by invasion and defeat at the hands of the Prussians among others. Then the danger had been overcome and remarkable victories had been won by a *levée en masse* – a rising up of the whole

See Preface for explanation of * symbol.

country in which armies of raw recruits, because of their courage and determination, had defeated the smaller but better trained armies of the invaders. The Government of National Defence decided to emulate their revolutionary predecessors.

Decisive action was needed because the situation was dire. The surrender at Sedan had removed one major French army, and the second had been surrounded at Metz. There was no danger of this army surrendering in the near future, but it was unable to take offensive action because Prussian artillery dominated the surrounding area. The way was thus open for the Prussian troops which had been victorious at Sedan to march on Paris, and it was well understood that if Paris fell it would be very difficult to continue the war.

## a) The Siege of Paris

Paris, however, was well defended by a ring of strong fortresses, and so many troops were in the capital that any attack was thought certain to fail. The government imagined that as the perimeter of the fortresses was so great – 61 kilometres – it would be impossible for the Prussians to surround Paris as they had Metz. Nevertheless, the Government took full precautions. The capital was crammed full of food, equipment and men. It was believed that whatever the Prussians did now, they could not be victorious.

To the great surprise of the Government, the Prussians, helped by troops from their south German allies, *were* able to lay siege to Paris. Within three weeks of the surrender at Sedan, Paris was completely cut off, encircled by 250 000 troops along an 80-kilometre front (thus keeping out of range of the guns in the fortresses). But the French were not dismayed. They knew that the Prussians dared not attack Paris, garrisoned as it was by more than 400 000 troops with more than 3000 heavy guns, and that the capital could hold out for several months before hunger would induce surrender. They believed there would be ample time for new armies to be recruited in the provinces and to march to raise the siege.

However, things did not go well. Gambetta, a member of the Government of National Defence, was sent from Paris to organize resistance in the provinces. His escape from Paris in a hot-air balloon – one of the 65 that carried news out of Paris during the siege – caught the public imagination, but despite heroic efforts on his part to organize new armies, the time had passed when largely untrained troops could hope to win victories over battle-hardened opponents. Some small successes were achieved but the Prussians were able to deal with the new armies Gambetta raised without having to relax their grip on Paris.

It seemed that the Parisians would have to find their own salvation. This they were sure they could do. It seemed obvious to them that because the number of troops inside Paris greatly outnumbered those besieging it, and because those inside the city could choose exactly which part of the perimeter to attack, a well-organized break-out must be successful. As the weeks passed and little happened, the people of Paris began to suspect treachery on the part of their government. The demand for military action became irresistible despite the fact that the military commanders realized it must end in defeat. Not only were many of the troops in Paris relatively poorly trained and ill-disciplined, but it was virtually impossible to mass troops ready for a break-out without the enemy, from their observation posts, knowing exactly what was happening. Even had the French been able to organize a surprise attack, the Prussians had dug themselves in so well and in such depth, with all the approaches to their positions well covered by artillery, that attacking troops were likely to be dispersed before they reached the enemy lines. Despite this, attacks were mounted against the besieging forces. It was the only hope the Government had of avoiding a revolution against itself. Each of the attacks ended in failure.

By Christmas many Parisians had come to the conclusion that there was no real alternative to surrender. When, in early January, the Prussians began a heavy bombardment of the city, concentrating on the perimeter fortresses but still launching between three and four hundred shells per night into built-up areas, the will to resist had largely evaporated. If anything the bombardment stiffened resistance a little, but the end could not be long delayed. On 28 January 1871 Paris capitulated. An armistice was signed to allow elections to be held for an Assembly that would be empowered to make peace with Prussia, or Germany as it had now come to be called, for ten days earlier the King of Prussia had been declared the Emperor of Germany. The fact that this ceremony had taken place in the Palace of Versailles, the symbol of France's greatness under the Bourbon Kings, was the final humiliation for the French.

## b) The Treaty of Frankfurt

Worse was to come. Germany was in a position to dictate the terms of peace. Much of France was occupied, all was war-weary, and there were no armies to continue the struggle. Bismarck could ask for what he wanted and France was in no position to object. When the terms Germany was imposing became known, it was seen just how harsh they were. A huge war indemnity was demanded, far higher than had ever been sought before, and so high that most commentators in Europe considered it beyond France's ability to pay.

The final treaty stated:

1   The payment of 500 million francs shall be made within thirty days after the re-establishment of the authority of the French Government in the City of Paris. One billion shall be paid in the course of the year, and 500 million on the first of May, 1872. The
5   last three billion shall remain payable on the second of March,

1874, as stipulated in the Preliminary Treaty. From the second of March of the present year the interest of those three billion francs shall be paid each year on the third of March, at the rate of 5 per cent per annum.

10   All sums paid in advance of the last three billion shall cease to bear interest from the day on which the payment is made.

The payment can be made only in the principal German commercial towns, and shall be made in metal, gold, or silver, in Prussian Bank notes, in Netherlands Bank notes, in notes of the

15   National Bank of Belgium, in first-class negotiable bills to order, or letters of exchange, payable at sight.

The German Government having fixed in France the value of a Prussian Thaler at 3 francs 75 centimes, the French Government accepts the conversion of the moneys of both countries at the rate

20   above stated.

After the payment of the first 500 million and the ratification of the definitive Treaty of Peace, the *départements* of the Somme, Seine Inférieure, and Eure shall be evacuated in so far as they shall be found to be still occupied by German troops. The evacuation of

25   the *départements* of the Oise, Seine-et-Oise, Seine-et-Marne, and Seine, as well as the forts of Paris, shall take place so soon as the German Government shall consider the reestablishment of order, both in France and Germany, sufficient to ensure the execution of the engagements contracted by France.

30   Under all circumstances, the evacuation shall take place after the payment of the third 500 million.

France was also required to give to Prussia the whole of Alsace and a large part of Lorraine. These large areas, with a population of more than 1½ million, had long been thought of as an integral part of France and there was no desire on the part of the people to be joined to Germany. Yet there could be no choice in the matter. By the Treaty of Frankfurt, which officially brought the Franco–Prussian War to a close, Alsace–Lorraine became a part of Germany. That the area contained much of France's iron ore and was the centre of the French textile industry was important, but not nearly so important to most French people as the feeling that their country had been raped. The desire for *revanche* (revenge) was to be a strong undercurrent in French history during the next 50 years. Germany had been firmly established as the national enemy, with whom there would at some time be a day of reckoning.

## 2 The Paris Commune

When Paris had surrendered the Prussians had agreed to a cease-fire throughout the country so that elections could be held. Bismarck was shrewd enough to realize that if he made peace with the Government of National Defence, a government that had seized power rather than having been elected, there was a real possibility that the terms would subsequently be repudiated by a properly elected government. He wanted to be sure that he was making peace with people who adequately represented the whole of France. Because the elections were organized in a hurry – they took place less than a fortnight after the capitulation of Paris – there was little time for candidates to conduct a proper campaign. In most districts it was a matter of choosing between peace and a continuation of the war. There was no question of the election being fought on party political lines, for no national parties existed with a machinery that could be brought into action so speedily. It seems that throughout the country, outside the large cities, a similar pattern emerged. Local dignatories, especially from long-established wealthy families which had kept their distance from the regime of Napoleon III, presented themselves for election with a policy of peace and public order. They were elected in a vast majority of cases.

The National Assembly that met in Bordeaux in February 1871 certainly was a faithful reflection of the nation's desire for peace at almost any price. It was well understood that there was little room for manoeuvre with the Prussians and that there was no likelihood of being able to escape the twin demands of the ceding of Alsace–Lorraine and the payment of an enormous indemnity, for only after these demands had been met would Prussian troops withdraw from France. So there was little disagreement over the terms of the Treaty of Frankfurt; they were extremely painful but there was no realistic alternative.

In other ways, however, the Assembly did not accurately represent the mood of the country. As most Deputies had been voted for largely because they were in favour of peace and were men of local importance, their views on many issues, especially on the form of government by which France should be ruled, had not been of great significance in the eyes of the electorate. So, almost by chance, it transpired that a clear majority in the National Assembly supported a restoration of the monarchy, although there were deep divisions over whether it should be the Bourbon Monarchy that had been deposed in 1830 or the Orleanist Monarchy that had been overthrown in 1848. So that a dispute over political systems should not hold up the work of the Assembly in making decisions on other important matters, it was agreed that for the time being the Deputies would elect a government but would not commit themselves in any way to a particular type of regime. Adolphe Thiers, the elder statesman aged 73 who had first made his mark politically as a leader of the loyal opposition to Louis-Philippe in the 1840s, was asked to lead the government and was given the title of 'Chief of the Executive Power'. He gathered around him a collection of ministers drawn from all political points of view, except the extreme Left.

## a) The Causes of the Commune

Thiers and his ministerial colleagues identified the restoration of normality as being the most urgent task to be undertaken. They saw that while economic dislocation continued there would be no prospect of raising the sums of money demanded by the Prussians. They were also aware that social revolution tends to go hand in hand with economic disruption, and, as men of wealth and property, they were determined to resist any demands for social change from the lower orders. They were naturally very suspicious of Paris. Starting with the Revolution of 1789 and continuing in 1814, 1830, 1848 and 1870, the capital had dictated to the rest of the country a change in the system of government. To the conservative men from the provinces it seemed that Paris was a barely governable hotbed of political and social discontent which must not be allowed to dominate events in the future. So, when the ending of hostilities with Prussia made it safe for the Assembly to move from Bordeaux, the decision was taken not to move to Paris but to go instead to Versailles, 22 kilometres south of the city and out of range of the potentially riotous mobs.

This was a cause of concern to the people of Paris, as was the determination of the Assembly to return to economic normality as speedily as possible and regardless of the consequences. During the war, and especially during the siege, it had been impossible for many people to continue earning their living as the majority of businesses had ceased to operate, having lost access to raw materials, markets or both. Many families had survived by withholding the payment of rent, by pawning the possessions they could temporarily do without, especially the tools of their trade, and by relying for income on the daily wage paid to those who enrolled in the National Guard. Shopkeepers and other small businessmen who had continued to operate had done so by utilizing a system of promissory notes which had allowed them both to extend and be extended credit.

In early March 1871 the Assembly voted to put an end to these economic irregularities. Rent that was owed was to be paid; goods deposited at the huge government-run pawnshop were to be sold unless they were redeemed speedily; payment of wages to the National Guard was to be stopped unless hardship could be proved; and promissory notes were to be honoured with cash once they became due (normally after six months). These measures almost equated to a declaration of war on Paris. People who had just undergone six months of hardship were now faced by the prospect of financial ruin and even homelessness.

Within a week of the Assembly's decision there were 150 000 declarations of bankruptcy in the capital as what for many people amounted to a lifetime's work was destroyed. Before this, there had been an obvious division between the Parisian 'haves' and 'have-nots', with the men of property clearly siding with the 'Party of Order'. Now it was more a matter of a division between Paris and the rest of the country, the Parisians, irrespective of wealth and social position, feeling that they were under attack. This new sense of unity in the capital was heightened by the absence of most of the richest ten per cent of the population who had escaped to the provinces either before the siege or immediately after it.

Thiers and his government were not unaware of what they were doing. Their dislike of the social and political unrest that Paris symbolized to them led to more than a determination not to be dominated by it; they actually looked forward to destroying Paris as a centre of revolutionary activity if the occasion arose. Thiers did not have long to wait. On 18 March an attempt was made by government troops to take away the 417 cannons that were still in the possession of the Parisian National Guard. The men sent to capture the 171 guns that were stored in a large 'gun-park' at the top of Montmartre hill were unable to complete their work as they had insufficient horses to drag the guns away. Angry crowds soon surrounded them, and in the face of this intimidation the soldiers lost the will to resist. The officers were captured by the crowd. The two generals in charge were murdered. Thiers' reaction was immediate. All government officials and troops were instructed to withdraw from the city in order to prepare for a re-entry in force. Those who remembered Thiers' advice to Louis-Philippe in 1848 to leave Paris and to return at the head of an army were not surprised at the decision of the Chief of the Executive Power. The Government had been spoiling for a fight and the events of 18 March merely provided the pretext. Unfortunately for France, the people of Paris were prepared to give as good as they got.

## b) The Establishment of the Commune

The Government's perception of Paris was not totally incorrect; it was merely exaggerated. There were in the city thousands of political activists who did not accept the prevailing social order and the political system which ensured that the rights of property and the desire to keep taxes low were always given precedence over the needs of the people, especially the need for healthy living and working conditions. These activists had organized themselves into political clubs, at which discussions about the changes that were needed and the way in which they could be best brought about took place. The clubs had even organized themselves into a city-wide federation which held meetings in an attempt – generally fruitless because of passionate disagreements – to co-ordinate their activities. But only a tiny minority of Parisians were members of political clubs. The Government over-rated their importance.

During the Siege almost every able-bodied man had joined the National Guard and a Central Committee of the National Guard had emerged as a vehicle for publicizing the views of the fighting men of Paris. The Government was correct in thinking that this organization had pretensions that outstripped its legal standing, for the Central Committee was dominated by men who hoped to capitalize on the dislocation of war in order to bring about social and political changes. Yet even here it was only a very small minority who were in any sense revolutionaries.

The events of 18 March, especially the withdrawal of all government personnel from Paris, left a vacuum of power that the activists were quick to fill. The Central Committee of the National Guard assumed control of the city and organized elections. These took place eight days later. The councillors who were elected wasted no time in declaring Paris a commune – an independent political entity owing allegiance to no-one. The hope was that other areas of France would establish their own communes, and that these would come together to form a federal state. The demands of the Communards were outlined in a placard that was pasted to walls in all parts of Paris in April.

1   . . . What do we ask?
      The recognition and strengthening of the Republic, which is the only government compatible with the rights of the people and the free and ordered development of society.
5     The absolute autonomy of the Commune extended to all districts of France, assuring integral rights to each district, and to every Frenchman the full exercise of his faculties and aptitudes, as man, citizen, and worker.
      The autonomy of the Commune shall have no limits other than
10  the right of autonomy equally enjoyed by all other communes adhering to the contract, and by whose association together French Unity will be preserved.
      The rights inherent to the Commune are: voting for the Communal budget, receipts and expenditure; fixing and
15  assessment of taxes; control of local services; organization of local magistrates, police and schools; administration of property belonging to the Commune.
      Selection by ballot or competition with the responsibility and permanent right of control and dismissal of magistrates and all
20  communal civil servants of all grades. Absolute guarantee of individual freedom, freedom of conscience, and freedom to work. Permanent intervention of citizens in communal affairs by the free expression of their ideas. Organization of urban defense and of the National Guard, which elects its leaders and is solely responsible
25  for the maintenance of order in the city.
      Paris asks nothing further in the way of local guarantees, on the understanding that the large central administration delegated by the federation of communes shall adopt and put into practice these same principles.
30    The Unity which has been imposed on us up to now by the Empire, the Monarchy, and Parliamentarianism is nothing but despotic centralization, and is unintelligent, arbitrary, and burdensome. The Political Unity which Paris desires is the

voluntary association of all local initiatives.

35   The Communal Revolution, begun by popular initiative on March 18, ushers in a new era of experimental, positive, scientific policy.

It spells the end of the old world with its governments and its clerics, militarism, officialdom, exploitation, stock-jobbing,
40   monopolies, and privileges to which the proletariat owes its servitude, the country its ills and its disasters.

Karl Marx wrote about the Commune in his pamphlet, *The Civil War in France*. He was in no doubt about what were the intentions of the Communards. They are clearly implied in his description of events written only a few weeks after they actually happened.

1   The first decree of the Commune was the suppression of the standing army, and the substitution for it of the armed people.

The Commune was formed of the municipal councillors, chosen by universal suffrage in various wards of the town, responsible and
5   revocable at short terms. The majority of its members were naturally working men, or acknowledged representatives of the working class. The Commune was to be a working, not a parliamentary body, executive and legislative at the same time. Instead of continuing to be the agent of the Central Government,
10   the police was at once stripped of its political attributes, and turned into the responsible and at all times revocable agent of the Commune. So were the officials of all other branches of the Administration. From the members of the Commune downwards, the public service had to be done at *workmen's wages*. The vested
15   interests and the representation allowances of the high dignitaries of State disappeared along with the high dignitaries themselves. Public functions ceased to be the private property of the tools of the Central Government. Not only municipal administration, but the whole initiative hitherto exercised by the State was laid into the
20   hands of the Commune.

Having once got rid of the standing army and the police, the physical force elements of the old Government, the Commune was anxious to break the spiritual force of repression, the "parson-power," by the disestablishment and disendowment of all
25   churches as proprietary bodies. The priests were sent back to the recesses of private life, there to feed upon the alms of the faithful in imitation of their predecessors, the Apostles. The whole of the educational institutions were opened to the people gratuitously, and at the same time cleared of all interference of Church and State.
30   Thus, not only was education made accessible to all, but science itself freed from the fetters which class prejudice and governmental force had imposed upon it.

The judicial functionaries were to be divested of that sham

independence which had but served to mask their abject
35 subserviency to all succeeding governments to which in turn, they
had taken, and broken, the oaths of allegiance. Like the rest of
public servants, magistrates and judges were to be elective,
responsible and revocable.

The Paris Commune was, of course, to serve as a model to all the
40 great industrial centres of France. The communal *régime* once
established in Paris and the secondary centres, the old centralized
Government would in the provinces, too, have to give way to the
self-government of the producers. In a rough sketch of national
organization which the Commune had no time to develop, it states
45 clearly that the Commune was to be the political form of even the
smallest country hamlet, and that in the rural districts the standing
army was to be replaced by a national militia, with an extremely
short term of service. The rural communes of every district were to
administer their common affairs by an assembly of delegates in the
50 central town, and these district assemblies were again to send
deputies to the National Delegation in Paris, each delegate to be at
any time revocable and bound by the *mandat impératif* (formal
instructions) of his constituents. The few but important functions
which still would remain for a central government were not to be
55 suppressed, as has been intentionally misstated, but were to be
discharged by Communal, and therefore strictly responsible
agents.

That these aspirations smacked more of idealism than of realism is
obvious, but they do not appear to be quite so ridiculous when it is
remembered that Parisians had grown up in an atmosphere of civic pride
based on a feeling that Paris was France, and that where the capital led
the provinces would follow. History had seemed to teach them that this
was so. However, there is no disputing the fact that, in behaving so
extremely, the Paris authorities played straight into the Government's
hands. Viewed from the provinces it was clear that the capital was in
rebellion and would have to be brought to heel.

## c) The Second Siege of Paris

For Paris to take up such an extreme position might have been
justifiable had a real degree of unity existed. But whereas a large majority
of the city's population appears to have agreed that the Government was
acting unreasonably towards them, there was no similar consensus about
what should be done in response. Even among the people elected to serve
on the Commune there were deep divisions and mutual distrust. As is
usual in such situations, the leaders of the Commune spent more time in
arguing among themselves than in taking decisive action. So very little
was in fact achieved. Some measures were passed aimed at improving
working conditions, and rent arrears were written off, but the expected

social and economic revolution did not take place. This was partly because of internal divisions within the Commune, but also because the Government at Versailles began the second Siege of Paris within a week of the establishment of the Commune. Energies were needed to organize defence and could not be spared to bring about social and economic change.

Few people within Paris could have imagined that the Government would act as decisively as it did. It was assumed that there would be a long stalemate during which the Commune would be able to establish itself as a workable form of government. Because of this no steps were taken to prevent the government troops leaving Paris. Nor was any attempt made to attack Versailles and to capture Thiers and the National Assembly. The government was left to make its plans in peace. Its first task was to reach an agreement with Bismarck that the army would be allowed to grow beyond the limits imposed by the armistice; then the additional troops had to be trained in the techniques of civil warfare. One advantage that Thiers had was an officer corps which sympathized with his objectives, for since 1848 there had been a marked shift to the right in the type of men who had trained to be army officers. Gone were the days when the army led the nation in revolutionary fervour. With a loyal military leadership, Thiers felt confident enough to put his Versailles troops in the field against the Communards remarkably rapidly.

Throughout the two months of fighting that followed, the pattern remained largely unaltered. The Versailles troops took few risks, always operating from numerical and tactical superiority. If their position was weak at any time, they waited patiently until they could strengthen it. As a matter of course they shot the prisoners they took. The Communards for their part were largely unorganized, lacked discipline, and showed a great unwillingness to serve anywhere but in the streets around their homes. Throughout April and the first half of May the Versailles forces made steady progress, breaching the outer defences and infiltrating the western *arrondissements* (districts) of the city. By 21 May the Government was ready to launch the final attack. There followed *la semaine sanglante* (the week of bloodshed) during which the dramatic events which contributed so largely to the legend of the Paris Commune were enacted.

In central Paris and in the working class districts large numbers of barricades were erected. Estimates vary greatly as to how many there were, but they must have numbered several hundred. Each one was high enough to shelter a standing man and many of them were constructed around a cannon. They were normally built of the small cubes of stone (called sets) of which the roads were made, topped by metal pavement grills. Many of these barricades were defended valiantly by men and women who preferred death to surrender. Unfortunately the barricades were not constructed according to any predetermined plan so it was often possible for the Versailles troops to outflank a well-defended

# FIGURES DU JOUR PAR BERTALL

PARIS CUIT DANS SON JUS.

*Bismarck and Thiers watch 'Paris stewing in its own juice'.*

position and attack it from the rear. In an effort to stop this happening the Communards set buildings on fire in the hope that the attackers would be blocked by walls of flame. This was rarely successful but it did heighten the drama of the situation and correspondents were able to write of 'the blazing city'. Several important buildings, including the *hôtel de ville*, were destroyed in this way, although stories of fires being started by revolutionary women, *les pétroleuses*, which were widely believed at the time are probably untrue. More significant than the destruction of property was the destruction of life, for it was this that had the real effect on subsequent French history.

Both sides provided martyrs for their cause which sympathetic propagandists made much of, both at the time and later. For the forces of law and order there were the hostages who were shot as the Commune came to an end. There were more than seventy of them, including leading churchmen such as the Archbishop of Paris, and they had originally been taken captive in the hope that they would provide a bargaining counter with the Government. When it became clear both that Thiers was not interested in negotiations and that the Commune was about to be overwhelmed, the bitter hatred of the Church and the desire for some revenge against the rich and powerful felt by many leading Communards resulted in the hostages being murdered in cold blood.

For the Commune the death toll was much greater. It cannot be known exactly how many were killed for no records were kept and the bodies were disposed of without ceremony in mass graves and in mass burnings, but realistic estimates put the figure at about 25 000. This compares with the 877 government troops who died, of whom exact records were kept. This great disparity was not, of course, due to normal military factors – in street-to-street fighting the attacker is likely to suffer greater losses than the defender – but was the result of action taken after resistance had effectively ceased, when the Versailles forces set about the task of hunting down and shooting anyone who looked as if they had been fighting on behalf of the Commune. Many were shot without questions being asked, especially if they had tell-tale powder burns on their right shoulders showing that they had recently fired a gun, but often it was enough just to be dirty, as at least one chimney-sweep found to her cost. Many more were rounded up for questioning, often as a result of the more than 40 000 denunciations that were made to the authorities, and after the briefest of examination by an officer, were assigned to one of two groups, those to be shot and those to be held prisoner. Even if they were spared at this stage they were not safe, for the prisoners were marched off to Versailles and those who could not keep up with the pace of the rest were killed. Just as officers throughout Paris were encouraged to take the law into their own hands, so the officers accompanying the prisoners acted just as they wished. One picked out all the grey-haired prisoners and ordered them to be shot on the basis that if they had not fought in 1871 they had probably done so during the June Days of 1848. Of the

50 000 who were eventually brought to trial nearly half were freed for there was no evidence against them. Those convicted were either transported (during which many died in appalling conditions) imprisoned in France, or executed if it could be shown that they had played some part, however remote, in murder.

## d) The Effects of the Commune

Within a very short time Paris appeared to be back to normal. Businesses started up again, the debris was cleared, and most of the buildings damaged by fire were restored, as far as possible, to their former condition. But the psychological scars were deep and lasting. Once again, as had happened after the Revolution and the reign of Napoleon I, not only Paris but the whole of France was divided into two mutually hostile groups. After 1871 you were either for the Commune and what it represented or you were against it. It was a long time before many people felt safe enough to occupy the middle ground between the two. In the meantime the majority of the French were confirmed in their relatively unthinking conservatism, convinced that the only alternative to the status quo was anarchy and revolution. Once again events had conspired to put off the time when change would be seen to be possible by peaceful political means. The Commune seemed to prove that it was revolution or nothing.

Not only did the events surrounding the Commune and its extinction further polarize political opinion in France, they also served to tip the balance in favour of the Right for the second time within a generation. In 1848 the left-wing activists had either been killed or imprisoned as the result of the abortive uprising in Paris known as the June Days. For much of the next twenty years supporters of the idea of a working-class political movement spent their time under lock and key. It was only in the final years of the reign of Napoleon III that there began to emerge in Paris, and other major cities such as Lyons and Marseilles, signs of the lower orders of society organizing themselves in the hope of improving their conditions by peaceful political means.

Between September 1870 (the fall of the Second Empire) and May 1871 (the destruction of the Commune) there was, of course, an explosive growth in working-class political activity. Thereafter it ceased. Nearly all the leading working-class thinkers, propagandists and organizers were either dead or imprisoned, and those who were not, found that their 'natural' supporters were in no mood to risk being identified with revolutionaries and trouble-makers. Even when an amnesty was granted in 1880 to all those Communards who were still in prison or in exile, it took some time for left-wing politicians to overcome a sense of 'once bitten twice shy' among the lower orders of society who had most to gain from change. Perhaps the long-term effects of the Commune can best be seen by comparing events in France with those in Germany, where universal manhood suffrage also existed. While socialism in France remained little discussed and poorly supported, the Socialist Party in Germany grew at such a pace that in the 1880s it was challenging for power and was seen by Bismarck as a major threat to the Prussian social and political systems. Yet it was in France that early socialist thinking had been developed and it is reasonable to think that, in Paris at least, it would have led the way in Europe had it not been for the Commune and the way it was put down. Thiers had intended to destroy the forces that were agitating for radical social change and he was largely successful.

Some historians have argued that the Commune, besides accentuating the divisions in French political life and inhibiting the growth of a working-class political movement, was of significance because it constituted a landmark in modern European history. Karl Marx, the founder of the branch of socialism we know as communism, saw in the Commune the first concerted attempt by the proletariat (working classes) to overthrow the forces of capitalism and to establish a social and political system based on working-class domination. Following this lead, Marxist historians have tended to interpret the Commune as the precursor of the Russian Revolution of 1917. Certainly there is sufficient evidence to prove that some of the Commune's leaders and some of the writers in the revolutionary press of Paris were convinced by Marx's theories and believed that they were partaking in a socialist revolution that would have far-reaching effects on the history of the world. However, it is clear that Communist ideas were just one of the multitude of strands of thinking that made up the confused ideology of the Commune. To attempt to see the events of March to May 1871 as a vindication of Marx's view of history is to stretch the evidence too far. If there were a single major cause of the Commune – and to suggest so is to risk huge oversimplification – it was a widespread sense of frustration and despair at the prospect of the pain and suffering of the Siege being added to by the decisions of an unsympathetic government. It seemed likely that an attempt would be made to put the clock back politically, rather than to capitalize on the disasters of the war by bringing about changes that seemed so obviously necessary.

---

*Making notes on 'The Franco–Prussian War and the Paris Commune, 1870–71'*

This chapter describes two 'events'. In each case you need to make an outline record of what happened, in chronological order and with a clear indication of the passage of time. For each step in the narrative you should be seeking causes (answers to the question, 'Why did this happen?'), and effects (answers to the question, 'What were the results of this?'). These should be noted.

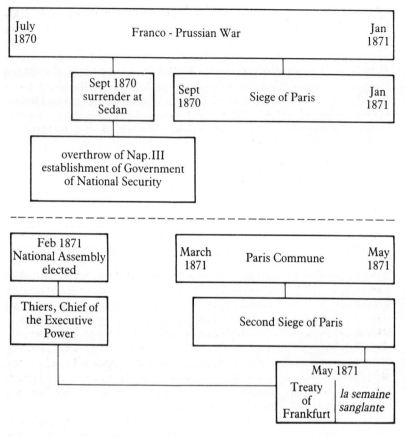

*Summary – The Franco–Prussian War and the Paris Commune*

The following headings and sub-headings should allow you to make appropriate notes:

1.    The Franco–Prussian War, (1870–71)
1.1.  Early defeats and the overthrow of the Second Empire
1.2.  The siege of Paris
1.3.  The Treaty of Frankfurt
2.    The Paris Commune, (1871)
2.1.  Background
2.2.  Causes
2.3.  The establishment of the Commune
2.4.  The second Siege of Paris
2.5.  Effects

*Answering essay questions on 'The Franco–Prussian War and the Paris Commune, 1870–71'*

The material from this chapter is most likely to be used when you write a general essay about the threats to the Republic and/or why the threats were overcome. The writing of general essays is discussed on pages 99–100. But occasionally you may be asked to write an essay that appears to concentrate on the war or the Commune.

Such essays tend to require a consideration of the importance/ significance/effects of these events. Typical examples are:

'How was France affected by her defeat at the hands of the Germans in 1870–1?' (London, 1979)
'Examine the consequences for France of defeat in the war of 1870–71.' (Oxford, 1984)
'What was the historical significance of the Paris Commune?' (AEB, 1982)
'What was the importance of the Paris Commune?' (Oxford, 1982)

When planning an answer to any question about the importance/ significance/effects of an event it is helpful to think of three chronological categories of effects: immediate, short-medium term, and long term. For each category it is helpful to make a list of the points you would wish to include. In the case of the immediate effects of the Franco–Prussian War these would be points such as the overthrow of the Second Empire; the economic dislocation, especially in those areas directly affected by the fighting; the loss of Alsace–Lorraine; and the election of a monarchist majority. You might find it helpful at this stage to make lists for the other chronological categories and for the Commune.

Once paragraph points have been chosen in this way, a decision has to be reached about the order in which they will be presented. This issue is discussed on pages 99–100.

---

*Source-based questions on 'The Franco–Prussian War and the Paris Commune, 1870–71'*

### 1 The Treaty of Frankfurt
Read carefully the extract from the Treaty of Frankfurt, given on pages 11–12. Answer the following questions:
a) What was the total size of the indemnity France was to pay (one billion equals one thousand million)?
b) What incentives were there for the French to pay the indemnity as speedily as possible?
c) What are the implications of the clauses about methods of payment and exchange rates? (lines 12–20)

## 2  The Aspirations of the Communards
Read carefully the extracts from the placard and from Marx's 'The Civil War in France', given on pages 16–18.

a)   The placard suggests that the Commune intended to bring about greater popular control of government. What were those controls?

b)   Both sources describe the intended system of national political organization to be adopted. What was this? In what ways do the two accounts differ? What are the likely reasons for these differences?

c)   The placard states the Communards' dislike of 'clerics, militarism, officialdom, exploitation, stock-jobbing, monopolies, and privileges', (lines 39–40). For three of these issues, describe what Marx says was done.

d)   What was Marx's attitude towards the Commune, as shown in the extract on pages 17–18? Give evidence to support your answer.

## 3  'Paris stewing in its own juice'
Study carefully the cartoon taken from Le Grelot and reproduced on page 20. Answer the following questions:

a)   What events is the cartoonist commenting on? Explain your answer.

b)   What is the cartoonist's attitude towards the people of Paris as suggested by evidence in the cartoon?

c)   How is Thiers depicted? What points is the cartoonist making by doing this? Explain your answer.

# CHAPTER 3

# Uncertainties Resolved, 1871–9

## 1 The Monarchists' Position

With the Commune defeated, Thiers and his ministers and the Deputies of the National Assembly could turn their attention to the issue that most filled their thoughts: the form of government France was to have. In theory the matter should have been speedily resolved; in practice it was very different. With over sixty per cent of the Deputies being supporters of a restoration of the monarchy, it was assumed in many parts of the country that their will would prevail. It was known that the Monarchists were deeply divided between the Legitimists and the Orleanists. The Legitimists advocated a return of the Bourbon family which had ruled France for centuries up to 1830 with only the break of the Revolution and Napoleon I, and the Orleanists championed the cause of the descendants of Louis-Philippe, who had been king from 1830 to 1848.

However, a ready solution to the problem seemed to exist. The Legitimists' hopes rested on the comte de Chambord, the grandson of Charles X, the King who had been forced to abdicate in 1830. Although Chambord was happily married, he had no children, and as he was over fifty it seemed unlikely that the situation would change. So when Chambord died the Bourbon line would come to an end and the Legitimists would need to transfer their allegiance to the nearest male relative. As chance would have it, this was no other than the comte de Paris, Louis–Philippe's grandson, whose claims to the throne were already supported by the Orleanists. So it did not seem beyond the bounds of possibility that the Orleanists would be prepared to support the Legitimists in order to ensure a restoration, in the certain knowledge that their candidate would in time become king.

At first it seemed that this was just the way things would be. The Orleanists, realizing that unless the Monarchists were united they would achieve nothing, were prepared to swallow their pride and accept that the claims of the comte de Chambord should be regarded as superior to those of the comte de Paris. Even the comte de Paris himself was willing to accept the authority of Chambord, and to swear loyalty to him in return for recognition as heir apparent.

* Yet there was a stumbling block. The comte de Chambord was only prepared to accept the crown on very particular terms. He had spent the last forty years in exile surrounded by faithful followers who had filled his head with notions of the importance of his destiny. They had convinced him especially of the role he was destined to play in righting the wrongs that had been perpetrated by successive governments of France, particularly during the Revolutionary and Napoleonic eras. As a result, Chambord was only prepared to be king if he could be assured that he would be able to cleanse France of its revolutionary legacy. Strangely enough he

was willing to accept all sorts of limitations on his powers which were suggested by his supporters in order to make a restoration acceptable to as wide a cross-section of society as possible. He raised no objection to being a constitutional monarch, working within the framework to be agreed between himself and the people's elected representatives. He could see no difficulty in adopting a parliamentary style of government which would virtually force him to appoint ministers who could command majority support in the National Assembly. He was even prepared to accept such democratic procedures as universal manhood suffrage. But he was adamant that he could never be the king of a country that had as its flag the *tricolore*, that most important symbol of the Revolution. His point of view was expressed in his manifesto to the people of France, published in July 1871.

1 PEOPLE OF FRANCE:

I am among you. You have opened the doors of France to me, and I could not refuse the happiness of again seeing my country, but I do not wish by staying longer to give new
5 pretexts for excitement in times as troubled as these.

I am therefore leaving this Château of Chambord which you gave me, and from which I took the name borne proudly for forty years along with the exile's path.

In going, I must tell you that I am not parting from you; France
10 knows I belong to her.

I cannot forget that royal legality is the heritage of the nation, nor can I refuse those duties to the nation which it imposes upon me.

These duties I shall fulfil, on my word as an honest man and as King.
15 With God's help we shall found together, whenever you wish, a government conforming to the real needs of the country, broadly based on administrative decentralization and local liberties.

As a guarantee of these public liberties to which every Christian people has a right, we shall grant universal suffrage honestly
20 practised, and authority to two Chambers; and we shall resume, restoring its true character, the national movement of the end of last century.

A minority in revolt against the country's wishes made it the beginning of a period of demoralization by falsehood and of
25 disorganization by violence. Their criminal schemes inflicted revolution on a nation which asked only for reform, and since then has driven it into an abyss in which, recently, it would have perished but for the heroic effort of our army.

It is the labouring classes, these workers in field and town whose
30 lot has been the subject of my liveliest concern and my dearest studies, who have suffered most from this social disorder.

But France, cruelly disabused by these unparalleled disasters,

will understand that one cannot return to the truth by an exchange
of errors; that eternal necessities cannot be evaded by expedients.

35   She will recall me and I shall come to her intact – with devotion,
my principle and my flag.

As regards the flag, it has been said that there are conditions to
which I cannot submit.

People of France! I am ready to do everything to help my country
40 to rise again from its ruins and to regain her position in the world;
the only sacrifice I cannot make for her is sacrifice of my honour.

I belong, and want to belong, to my time: I pay sincere homage
to all its greatness and, under whatever colour flag our soldiers
marched, I have admired their heroism and thanked God for all
45 that their courage added to the treasure-house of France's glory.

Between you and me there must be no misunderstanding, no
mental reservations.

No, I shall not – because ignorance and credulity have spoken of
privilege, absolutism or intolerance, and I know not what else, of
50 tithes, feudal rights, phantoms which the most daring bad faith is
trying to raise before your eyes – I shall not permit the standard of
Henry IV, of Francis I, and of Joan of Arc, to be snatched from my
hands.

It was under this flag that national unity was achieved, that your
55 fathers, led by mine, conquered Alsace and Lorraine, whose fide-
lity to us is still a consolation in our grief.

It conquered barbarism in that land of Africa, witness to the first
feats of arms of the princes of my family: it will conquer the new
barbarism that is menacing the world!
60   I shall entrust it without fear to the valour of our army. It has
always followed, as they know, only the path of honour.

I received it as a sacred trust from the old King, my grandfather,
when he died in exile. It has always been, for me, inseparable from
the memory of my absent fatherland. It floated over my cradle: may
65 it overshadow my grave.

In the glorious folds of this unsullied standard I shall bring you
order and liberty.

People of France! Henry V cannot abandon the white flag of
Henry VI.

In this, he was rightly taken seriously for the question of what flag
France should have was a matter of deep emotional importance to many
of his countrymen. Before 1789 the family emblem of the Bourbons, a
white flag with blue fleur-de-lis, had been the flag of France. During the
Revolution and the First Empire the victorious armies of France had
marched under the new flag of red, white and blue, the *tricolore*. Apart
from the brief Bourbon Restorations of 1814 to 1830, this had remained
the nation's flag ever since, and it symbolized to most people the fact that

they were free and equal members of the state with rights that nobody
was empowered to take away from them. In contrast, the white flag of the
Bourbons was a reminder of times when the country was the personal
property of one family, and when rights and liberties existed only in so
far as the King was prepared to grant them. To remove the people's flag
would be to remove one of the  things that most citizens identified with
most easily.

But the comte de Chambord was only able to view the issue from his
own standpoint. To him the *tricolore* symbolized all that had gone wrong
in France since 1789, especially a loss of respect for God, and for his
representatives on earth. For him to serve under this flag would be to
turn his back on all he thought he had been born to do. It was clearly a
real matter of principle which he saw as being of central importance. He
is reported as saying, 'Without principle I am just a fat man with a limp',
and in his terms he was right. Yet understandable as his position was, it
was highly frustrating to his more powerful supporters, many of whom
were politicians interested in restoring the monarchy rather than idealists
prepared to sacrifice all for the sake of a principle. Few of these men were
willing to accept that Chambord's position was immovable. So they set
about the business of persuading him that he could have both the essence
of his principle and the reality of political power.

## 2 Adolphe Thiers

In Adolphe Thiers France had found a leader who was more than
willing to fill the vacuum left by the provisional nature of the regime that
had been established after the overthrow of the Empire in September
1870. Apart from a few days at the end of Louis-Philippe's reign, he
had been out of power for more than thirty years. Now was the time to
enjoy the fruits of a lifetime of endeavour during which he had been
recognized as one of the most talented politicians of the period although
circumstances had dictated that he should remain in opposition, becoming almost a voice in the wilderness. At the age of 74 he was obviously an
old man, but he had lost little of his effectiveness as a speechmaker. He
could still argue a case with passion and authority, in such a way that
those who heard him could hardly fail to be convinced that here was an
extraordinary man and a natural leader.

The National Assembly elected in February 1871 was just the place for
Thiers to shine. Most of its members were new to politics, at least at a
national level, and had no allegiance to a ready-made leader in the
Assembly, for no parties with a formal structure existed. The competition for leadership was very slight in comparison with Thiers' great
standing because the leading politicians from the previous regime had
gone into rapid retirement and because the Republican leaders, such as
Gambetta, who had led the resistance against the Prussians after the
capture of Napoleon III had been rejected by an electorate greedy for

peace. It had been no surprise, therefore, when Thiers had been chosen to be Head of the Executive Power.

The new leader set about his task with an obvious determination to enjoy himself. Besides being France's effective Head of State, he was also an ordinary member of the National Assembly and as such was able to attend and speak in debates as and when he wished. Those who knew him well commented on how much he was in his element speaking at length on decisive points to an audience that, in the early months at least, hung on his every word. He also revelled in the opportunity to entertain lavishly. In fact, to some people it seemed that the open house that Thiers kept was grander than had been the court of the Emperor Napoleon III.

But what he really enjoyed was power. Of this, to begin with, there was no lack. With Prussian troops occupying a considerable part of the country, Paris for a time in rebellion, and a huge war indemnity to be paid, there was no shortage of opportunity for decision making. Thiers rose to the occasion splendidly. With great energy and skill he won the confidence of the German authorities in France, as well as of Bismarck in Berlin, and utilized it in ensuring that the occupation ran smoothly so that no excuse was given for additional punitive action. He even managed to deal with the Commune without provoking German intervention, because he was at all times able to give the impression that he was completely in control of the situation, and that thus Bismarck had nothing to fear. However, the clearest sign of the stability he was quickly bringing to a war-weary country was the ease with which the money needed to pay the war indemnity was borrowed from the ordinary people of France. Two loans were raised and on each occasion much more than was needed was forthcoming. This was a clear sign of confidence, for prudent men do not risk their hard won savings in making a loan unless they are certain that the debt will be honoured. Thiers was therefore able to negotiate a timetable of troop withdrawals with the Germans which was to result in the last soldier leaving in September 1873, much earlier than could have been hoped for when the peace treaty was signed.

* When Thiers had been chosen as leader it was assumed that as a good Monarchist he was merely 'holding the fort' until the restoration could take place. But as the months passed by and the comte de Chambord became more and more determined not to compromise his principle, unease began to spread among the monarchists who could see their carefully thought out plan falling apart. Thiers was one of the first to see that a restoration, even if it could be agreed, was unlikely to be success-ful. He recognized that although the elections in February 1871 had produced a large Monarchist majority, the country was not generally in support of a return to the days when France was ruled by a king. He knew that the votes for the monarchists had largely been the result of a strong desire for peace, of a rejection of the men of the Second Empire and of the continued struggle against Germany. His opinion was substantiated when over a hundred by-elections were held in July 1871

and all but a handful of the seats went to Republicans, including Gambetta. Although this influx of Republicans did not destroy the Monarchist majority in the Assembly, it gave those who were prepared to see, a clear indication of the mood of the country. This realization, along with growing suspicion about Chambord's likely style of kingship when and if he decided to accept the throne, made many Orleanists wonder whether they might be better off throwing in their lot with the more conservative Republicans. After all, many of the Orleanists were much more interested in seeing the development of a parliamentary type of government, with ministers reflecting the majority view in the Assembly, than they were in witnessing the return of the family of Louis–Philippe to the throne, and this was just what the conservative Republicans stood for.

In November 1872 Thiers at last made his position clear. Without consulting his supporters he announced that he was in favour of a continuation of the Republic. 'It exists. It is the legal government of the country; to replace it would be a revolution and the most dangerous kind of revolution.' Some Orleanists agreed with him, including, it was claimed, one of the sons of Louis–Philippe, but many of the monarchists in the National Assembly felt that they had been betrayed. They had given their support to Thiers; they had even given him the title of President of the Republic in August 1871 once it had been agreed that the present regime was provisional and that the National Assembly had the right to decide what the permanent system of government should be. Now he had joined the ranks of their opponents. Urged forward by their newly emerging leader, the duc de Broglie, the Monarchists were determined to have their revenge. Their chance came in May 1873 when at last they were able to convince enough Deputies that the time had come to be rid of the man who seemed to regard himself as indispensable. Thiers was defeated in the Assembly and at once resigned.

This time the Monarchists ensured that they chose a head of state who was unlikely to develop political ambitions of his own. They selected Marshal MacMahon, duc de Magenta. MacMahon, who was descended from one of the many Irish gentlemen who took service in the French army during the eighteenth century, had been one of Napoleon III's leading generals and had made his name in the Italian Campaign of 1859. By leading the Versailles forces which suppressed the Commune he had shown that he was prepared to be loyal to whichever regime was in control at the time. As an Orleanist at heart and as a man who disliked the limelight – having to be persuaded by his wife that his duty to his country was to accept the Presidency once it was offered to him – he seemed the ideal person to occupy the position of Head of State until the monarchy could be re-established. So the so-called 'Republic of the Dukes', with MacMahon, duc de Magenta, as President, and the duc de Broglie as Prime Minister, began.

## 3 The Monarchists in Power

In the second half of 1873 a sense of urgency overcame the Monarchists, among whom should now be numbered the growing minority of Bonapartists who had found their way into the Assembly, mainly as a result of by-elections. Until 1873 the Bonapartists had remained loyal to the ageing and ill ex-Emperor, but his death released them from their obligations and allowed them to become free agents in the complicated political games that were being played in the Assembly.

At the heart of the new manoeuvrings was the feeling on the part of the leading supporters of a restoration that time was running out. It was clear that what popular support there was for the monarchy was disappearing fast as people lost confidence that anything would ever happen. What was worse, the trickle of by-elections that had taken place since July 1871 had confirmed that it was very difficult for the Monarchists to win in popular contests. There was now a real prospect of the Monarchist majority disappearing in the Assembly, reduced through by-elections and by the desertion of moderate Orleanists, like Thiers, who were throwing in their lot with moderate Republicans.

The duc de Broglie, confident as a result of a number of political deals that he could deliver a majority vote in favour of the restoration of Chambord as Henri V, set about the search for a compromise that would be acceptable to both the monarch-to-be and his supporters. A series of groups of negotiators made their way to Chambord's home, a castle in Austria, in order to explore ways in which progress could be made. Each group foundered on the issue of the flag, until at last the news was brought back to Paris that a solution had been found. Chambord, it was reported, had agreed to be restored under the *tricolore* and to leave it to the National Assembly to decide subsequently what should be the flag of France for the future. The Monarchists were jubilant. Preparations were put in hand for the triumphal entry of the new king into Paris, including the ordering of a new coach and appropriate decorations. Then disaster struck. Chambord realized that he had been misunderstood. When he had agreed to the form of words that had been received with joy by his supporters at home, he had done so on the understanding that the Monarchist majority in the National Assembly would do as he wished and vote for the Bourbons' white flag. Now the impression was being given publicly that he had agreed to accept the *tricolore* if that was what the people wanted. Nothing could have been further from his mind and he felt obliged to publish a statement repeating his decision that he would never serve under the *tricolore*. Coming after his supporters had already begun to celebrate their victory, this was a devastating blow. All those involved realized that the end of the road had been reached and that it was now certain that the last of the Bourbons would live and die a private citizen. They rapidly looked around for new hope.

\* There was no question of the crown being offered to somebody else.

The Legitimists were as immovable over this as Chambord had been over the flag. Either France must have its rightful king or France must have no king at all. As Chambord would not renounce his claims there was no room for manoeuvre by his supporters, so Broglie and the other Monarchist leaders could only search for a tactic that would leave the issue of the nature of the regime unresolved for as long as possible in the hope that death would clear the way for the comte de Paris. Their decision was to extend the presidency of MacMahon for a further seven years. This was done in November 1875, which, it was thought, would give breathing space until the end of the decade.

The Monarchists were, however, deluding themselves. Any real prospect of a restoration had in fact already disappeared. Even had a willing candidate been available, and even had a majority of the National Assembly voted in his favour, he is unlikely to have remained king for long, for the Monarchists were now so unpopular among large sections of society that rebellions would almost certainly have followed any restoration. This state of affairs had arisen largely because the Monarchists, who in early 1871 had appeared as bringers of peace and protectors against the possibility of social revolution, had by late 1873 gained the reputation of being warmongers and reactionaries. The issue that had done most to destroy their position as a potentially unifying force in France was the question of the Pope's temporal power.

Until 1870 the Pope had been the ruler of a state as well as head of the Catholic Church. The amount of territory he controlled had been greatly reduced when Italy was united in 1860. His domain had been limited to the area around Rome, which he had retained only thanks to the support of the French troops. In 1870 even this had been taken from him when the French had withdrawn in order to concentrate on the war with Prussia, and the Italian army had marched into Rome. Many of the Monarchists in France were also fervent Catholics and believed that the Pope, as God's representative on earth, should have temporal as well as spiritual powers. They saw it as their duty to take action to return to papal control what had been taken away by the Italians, especially as the Pope had shut himself up in the Vatican in Rome as a protest against the seizure of his land, and had announced that he would not move from his self-imposed imprisonment until what was rightfully his was returned to him. So there was much talk of France declaring war on Italy in order to come to the Pope's rescue. Although there was little likelihood that this would happen, especially as it was known that Bismarck was sympathetic to the Italian government's position, the anti-clerical feelings of much of the bourgeoisie and the urban working classes were brought to the surface once again. In the event, nothing was done to help the Pope.

The close identification of the monarchical cause with the interests of the Catholic Church was reinforced by the stance taken by the Government over the religious revival that was taking place. As had happened before in France, one element within the Church interpreted the national humiliation of defeat in war as a sign of God's displeasure with what had been happening in the country, and campaigned for a change in public morals and the taking of official decisions that would indicate the nation's repentance. Huge pilgrimages to places of religious importance within France were organized and received the blessing of ministers. A plan was devised to build a symbol of France's repentance, the basilica of Sacré Coeur on the hill of Montmartre in Paris. Government support was freely given, and in terms which showed that there was official support for the thinking that lay behind the scheme. And so the Monarchists who could have presented themselves as the people to heal the political wounds of the past, fell into the trap of becoming identified with only one part of French society, and one that was renowned for its extreme views. The middle ground of politics had been vacated and it was available to be filled by someone else.

The Monarchists' position was further weakened by their leaders, who lacked public appeal and any real flair for politics. MacMahon, as President, was straightforward and reliable but he was no politician. Issues tended to be black or white and the art of compromise was largely unknown to him. Unlike Thiers he was not a member of the National Assembly and this, coupled with his personality and experience, tended to mean that he was somewhat remote from the reality of day-to-day politics. He was thus more of a figure-head than a leader.

The Monarchists therefore had to rely on the duc de Broglie for leadership, for he was in effect the Prime Minister, although the post did not exist as such. Broglie had many virtues. He was hardworking, cared passionately about the cause he supported, was intelligent, courageous, and had the ability to put together a convincing argument. He was not, however, popular either with those who knew him or with those who only heard about him by report. To those who had regular contact with him, such as the Deputies in the National Assembly, he appeared haughty and unapproachable. He was the head of an ancient noble family and had been brought up to keep people at a distance. It was not that he was consciously a snob; it was just that he gave the appearance of being one. His natural reserve combined with an unfortunate quality of voice – a political opponent claimed that he spoke as other men gargled – made him a less than distinguished public speaker, and he could do little to bolster the morale of his supporters when they were under heavy attack in debate. As a publicist and a promoter of a cause to the nation he was inept. He had little idea of the thoughts and feelings of ordinary people, and thus could not start to work out strategies for appealing to them in terms that would be effective. He came over to the country as a man of the past who had little to offer in terms of solving the problems of the future.

## 4 The Constitution

To his credit, Broglie recognized his own shortcomings and was under no illusions about his and his supporters' chances in a general election. So once it became clear in November 1873 that the restoration was not imminent, it was important to get on with the task of providing France with permanent organs of state before the Monarchist majority disappeared. The intention was to establish a system that would give a built-in advantage to the conservative forces of the Right while remaining flexible enough to be converted to a monarchy at the opportune time. At first the pace was slow. At the same time as MacMahon had been given a seven-year term of office, a Commission had been set up to make recommendations on permanent institutions, but it proceeded at a very gentle pace.

The process might have dragged on for years had there not been an alarming – to Monarchists and Republicans alike – increase in popular support for the Bonapartists. This had been brought about by the emergence of Napoleon III's son, the Prince Imperial, as a young man of considerable public appeal. He was a much more attractive proposition for a restoration than was the stiff, starchy and middle-aged comte de Chambord. It was no wonder that the Bonapartists in the National Assembly swiftly disassociated themselves from the unsuccessful manoeuvrings of their fellow Monarchists and started to prepare for a return to power on their own account. In these circumstances it was in the interests of both the Monarchists and the Republicans to reach a decision reasonably speedily. So the Commission was prevailed upon to complete its deliberations and to present its report in January 1875.

There followed a series of new laws that together made up the Constitution of 1875, although there was no single constitutional document as there had been with each of the earlier nineteenth-century French regimes. The Monarchists hoped to be able to leave unresolved the question of a name for the permanent system of government that was now being established. It was true the word 'Republic' featured in the current system – there was after all a President of the Republic – but this was only a provisional regime. The Monarchists did not want to see a permanent Republic in France. Equally, the Republicans were determined that the Republic should be formally recognized.

The trial of strength came early in the proceedings, when Wallon, a Republican Deputy, proposed an amendment to the bill under discussion. He suggested the inclusion of a simple form of words, 'The President of the Republic is elected by the plurality of votes cast by the Senate and the Chamber of Deputies united as a National Assembly.' This amendment, known as the Wallon Amendment, was hotly debated because both sides recognized the significance of the word 'Republic'. In the end a number of moderate right-wing Deputies decided to vote with the Republicans as they could see little sense in refusing to accept what already existed, for MacMahon was and would continue to be the President of the Republic. The Amendment was passed by 353 votes to 352. Historians have made much of the fact that the Third Republic was properly brought into being with a majority of one vote. It was, in fact, not quite as dramatic as that. The National Assembly in 1875 still contained a majority of Deputies who hoped to see a return to one of the earlier regimes (monarchy or empire) and over the Wallon Amendment they were merely disagreeing about what should be the interim arrangements.

\* Yet as far as the Republicans were concerned a great victory had been achieved. They had made their point that no practical alternative to a republic existed, and they were confident that, despite the day-dreams of the Legitimists, Orleanists, and Bonapartists, the situation would not change in the future if they played their cards properly. It was fortunate that they were so pleased with this early success because on all other constitutional points they were defeated. They were especially displeased by the way in which the Right was setting up a system that was designed to give them a permanent stranglehold on power. The view of the Republicans was that the one-chamber National Assembly made up entirely of popularly elected Deputies which existed at the time should continue. They also supported the idea that there should be a President responsible to the Assembly, whether he was elected by universal suffrage or by the Deputies themselves. This, they felt, would ensure the purest possible form of democracy. But the system as established by the laws of 1875 was designed to be anything but pure democracy, which was something deeply distrusted by most Monarchists who were élitists, assuming that men of breeding, wealth, and worldly experience should run the country's affairs. They feared that if the common people were given effective power they would use it to further their own ends at the expense of their betters.

So the Monarchists planned to introduce a political system that would limit the powers of the Chamber of Deputies by making it share control of events with two other institutions, the Senate and the Presidency. It was hoped that if, as expected, the Chamber of Deputies contained a Republican majority after the next election, a right-wing Senate and a right-wing President would be more than a counterbalance. After all, it would be two against one. Thus, although the Monarchists had lost over the Wallon Amendment, they were confident that if they could have their way over the Senate and the Presidency all would be well. Therefore they were more than pleased by what was established by the constitutional laws of 1875.

The Senate was established to be as powerful as the Chamber of Deputies and was to be composed in such a way that a large right-wing majority seemed assured for evermore. Of its 300 members, 75 were to be elected for life by the current National Assembly, which should ensure a core of loyal Monarchists. The remaining 225 members were to be indirectly elected. So there would be no popular election. Instead, electoral colleges would be convened in each *département*, made up of one representative from each local government district whether it was a large city or a village, and these would elect the Senators. So electoral power would be overwhelmingly in the hands of the conservative countryside, at the expense of the more progressive urban areas. Senators would serve for nine years, with 75 retiring every three years in rotation. Thus any change in public opinion would take a very long time to be reflected in the nature of the majority in the Senate.

Equally, the arrangements made for the Presidency seemed to be very much in the interests of the Monarchists. The President was to be elected for seven years by simple majority vote of the Chamber of Deputies and the Senate sitting together. As it could be safely assumed that the Senate would contain a large majority of Monarchists who would be sure to out-vote any Republican majority in the Chamber of Deputies, there seemed no prospect of a President being elected who was not sympathetic to the monarchical cause. What is more, the President would be a powerful figure. He would be able to choose his own ministers and veto bills with which he did not agree. He would even be able to dissolve the Chamber of Deputies if he could obtain the agreement of the Senate.

Even in the arrangements made for the election of the Chamber of Deputies changes were made which were intended to give the Right some advantage. Instead of elections being by *scrutin de liste*, in which each elector voted for as many candidates as there were Deputies in his *département*, they were to take place in single member constituencies, a system called *scrutin d'arrondissement*. The hope was that this would reduce the power of those who were best organized – often Republican groups who had shown themselves more able to present the electors with an appealing list of candidates for a *département* than had been the Monarchists – and increase the likelihood of a local dignatory being elected. It was assumed, correctly, that local dignatories tended to be quite conservative. It was also agreed that for a candidate to be elected he must receive a majority of the votes cast. If nobody was in this position, a second ballot would be held a week later in which the two candidates who had received most support in the election would engage in a straight contest. It was thought that the Right had most to gain by this arrangement as it seemed that there was a 'natural' conservative majority in most constituencies, although this might be split between rival candidates to begin with.

## 5 The Triumph of the Republicans

Within four years of this structure being erected to protect the interests of the Monarchists, it was clear that it had almost totally failed. Even to begin with all did not go well. The election of the life members of the Senate was mishandled by Broglie and to his great surprise he found as the voting proceeded in the National Assembly that he had been outma-noeuvred by an unholy alliance of Republicans and Bonapartists who had combined to frustrate his wishes. Instead of 75 loyal Monarchists finding themselves with a seat in the Senate for life, 57 Republicans and 18 Bonapartists were chosen. This, however, was not as disastrous as it might seem, for in the elections to the Senate held in January 1876 the expected huge majority for the Right emerged, which more than swamped the Republicans among the life members. But it was a sign of how far opinion had shifted since 1871 that there were only two Legitimists among them.

The expected triumph of the Republicans in the election of Deputies duly took place in February and March 1876. Because there were no tightly organized political parties it is not possible to determine the exact strength of the rival groupings in the Chamber, but it seems that about two-thirds of those elected were committed to a continuation of Republican forms of government. Of the forces of the Right about half were Bonapartists, with many of the rest being Orleanists. There were no more than 30 Legitimists in a Chamber of 533 members.

The Right, however, hoped that MacMahon would be able to continue to pursue policies that were in their favour. As President he was in a strong position to determine the approach to be followed, for he could choose, and replace if necessary, all the ministers of the Government. He could also rely on the wholehearted support of the Senate, and so, it was thought, should be able to negate the Republican majority in the new Chamber of Deputies. But it did not work like this. The Republican leaders, especially Gambetta, were able to claim that as the only popularly elected representatives of the people they should decide the policies to be followed by the Government. At first MacMahon attempted to find a compromise solution that recognized the majority grouping in the Chamber but which resulted in the adoption of conservative approaches. For a time he was even prepared to have one of the Republican leaders, Jules Simon, as his Prime Minister. Yet it was unlikely that such a precarious balance would last for long, for while both MacMahon and the Republican leaders aspired to be the major force in the land and felt that they were in a strong position to win any struggle for power, the apparent harmony could only be shortlived. The showdown came in 1877. In what is known as the Crisis of *Seize Mai* (the sixteenth of May), MacMahon dismissed his Republican ministers when they failed to support the President's standpoint on religious matters in the Chamber, and replaced them with Monarchists led, once again, by Broglie.

Here was a constitutional issue to be tested, for although MacMahon was acting within his legal powers, and in a way that the constitution-makers of 1875 had envisaged, he was following a course that was most likely to end in political stalemate. He undoubtedly had the right to select ministers who were to his liking. But the majority in the Chamber were equally within their rights to refuse to support any of the measures put forward by these ministers. Such a situation could not be allowed to continue for long. MacMahon had either to gain a majority that was sympathetic to him in the Chamber, or he had to give way. He decided to use the power to dissolve the Chamber that had been invested in the President, with the Senate's approval, by the constitutional laws of 1875. In what had become a tradition of election-making since 1815, the whole machinery of government was brought into operation in an attempt to ensure that candidates who were supporters of the President were successful. In each constituency an 'official candidate' was put forward and was given a huge amount of free publicity through official publications. Much as he disliked it, MacMahon even toured the country speaking on behalf of the candidates of the Right.

In response the Republicans presented a united front, although there were great differences between those who wanted to maintain the social status quo and those who hoped for radical change, and fought the election as far as possible on the issue of parliamentary government. Their contention was that there could only be a proper form of parliamentary government if the ministers of the day were obliged to win majority support in the Chamber of Deputies, for it was only the Chamber of Deputies that could be thought of as representing the will of the people. The result of the election was decisive. Despite all the efforts of officialdom, less than half of those who voted were prepared to support the government, and the Republicans only lost ten per cent of the seats they had won a year earlier. They could still claim to hold a majority in the Chamber.

The parallels with the events of 1829–30 were very obvious to people at the time, for then, as well, the country's leader (in this case Charles X) had been faced with a parliamentary majority that would not support his choice of ministers. In both cases an appeal had been made to the electorate over the head of the existing Chamber of Deputies, and in both cases the government had failed to win a vote of confidence. Charles X had refused to accept the verdict of the voters and had attempted a *coup d'état* by which the electoral rules were changed so as to assure him of support in the future. This had led to a revolution in Paris and to the overthrow of the regime. People naturally began to wonder whether the same was about to happen 47 years later. Gambetta did not think so. In a letter written to a political associate he attempted to read MacMahon's mind.

1   There are several expedients open to him: they will at least occur to him, even if they are not feasible.
1. Attempt a show of strength. I don't believe he will, for very good reasons which I don't need to list to you, but the chief one is
5   this: the army is loyal and its *leaders* very divided, so it is impossible to risk such a step without being sure of being obeyed by *all*. So they will circulate these rumours, but not even the most timid people will be taken in by them. You can be sure that we have taken even stronger precautions than in 1873 to foil such an attempt if it
10  were made.

2. Try to patch up the differences between the Left-Centre and Right-Centre, so as to look like constitutional repentance. This expedient is more disquieting than the first, but thanks to the animosity of M. Thiers, and his authority over the section of the
15 Left which might weaken, there is no serious cause for fear; from which it should be plain to you, apart from other excellent reasons, how important it was to promote M. Thiers as candidate for the Presidency.

3. Capitulate and submit to all the conditions of the new majority.
20 An improbable solution, but one which certain people do not regard as impossible.

4. Resign. I think it will be this, in spite of all appearances, for I am convinced that the effect of the elections will be overwhelming and menacing for him.

MacMahon was very different from Charles X. Whereas the last of the Bourbon kings had been full of confidence that he was right and that in a crisis the people would support him, wrongly as it turned out, the second President of the Third Republic could see that the logic of the argument was on the side of his opponents, and that if he forced the issue he was likely to stir up just the revolutionary forces that he was determined to keep submerged. In the circumstances, the sensible thing to do seemed to be to give way with as good a grace as possible and hope that if he was losing the power to decide the direction in which France was to move, he was at least retaining the negative power of ensuring that events did not move too far in the wrong direction. So Broglie was dismissed and ministers were appointed who were able to win the support of the new Chamber. MacMahon offered an explanation of his actions in a letter to the Presidents of the Senate and of the Chamber of Deputies.

1 SIRS,
The elections of October 14 have once more confirmed the confidence of the country in its Republican institutions.

In obedience to parliamentary rules, I have formed a Cabinet
5 chosen from both Chambers, composed of men who are determined to uphold and maintain these institutions by wholehearted application of the Constitutional Laws.

It is imperative in the interests of the country that the present crisis should be resolved; it is no less imperative that the crisis
10 should not occur again.

Exercise of the right of dissolution is, after all, no more than a method of final consultation with a judge from whom there is no appeal, and could not develop into a system of government. I have felt bound to avail myself of this right, and I am complying with the
15 country's answer.

The Constitution of 1875 established a parliamentary Republic by laying down my nonresponsibility, whereas it instituted the

collective and individual responsibility of ministers. Thus our
respective duties and our rights are determined for us; the
20  independence of ministers is the precondition of their responsibility. These principles derive from the Constitution and are those of
my Government.

The end of this crisis will be the beginning of a new era of
prosperity. All the public powers will cooperate to encourage its
25  development. The agreement that has been reached between the
Senate and the Chamber of Deputies (which can now be confident
of reaching the end of its mandate in accordance with the regu-
lations) will enable the important legislative business required in
the public interest to be completed.

30  The Universal Exhibition will soon be opened; commerce and
industry will make rapid strides and we shall provide the world
with further testimony of the vitality of our country, which has
always recovered by hard work, thrift, and our deep respect for the
ideas of conservation, order and liberty.

Marshal de MacMahon

The fact that the new ministers were moderate men who, although
favouring Republican forms of Government, were only prepared to bring
about changes slowly, did much to convince even the conservative
sections of society that the Republic was the safest form of government
available to France at the time. Such was the extent of acceptance of the
new regime that the indirect election of Senators that took place in 1879
yielded a majority of Republican supporters. To MacMahon this was the
final straw. He felt that his rejection by the nation was now complete.
With something of a sense of relief he resigned. The pretensions of the
Monarchists were now at an end. The Republicans already controlled the
Chamber of Deputies and the Senate. They were now able to elect one of
their own number, Jules Grévy, as President. Nobody could realistically
doubt that the Third Republic had arrived to stay. It had begun life as the
obvious replacement of the defeated. Napoleon III; it had survived its
infancy because its opponents, although in power, could not bring about
the only alternative they could agree on; it had reached maturity as the
form of government that could attract the support of a majority of the
nation's voters. The question now was, what sort of Republic would it
turn out to be.

---

**Making notes on** *'Uncertainties Resolved, 1871–9'*

This chapter describes the Monarchists' attempts to bring about the
restoration of a king to France. The reasons for their failure are examined, and the triumph of the Republicans is explained. In each case you
are seeking answers to the questions, 'What happened?' and 'Why?'.

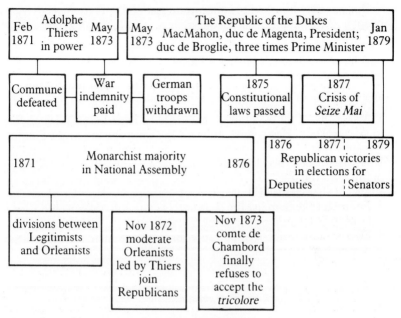

*Summary – Uncertainties Resolved, 1871–79*

The following headings and sub-headings will provide a suitable framework for your notes:
1. The monarchists' position
1.1. Orleanists
1.2. Legitimists
2. Adolphe Thiers
2.1. Achievements
2.2. Fall
3. The monarchists in power
3.1. Chambord
3.2. Unpopularity of the Monarchists
4. The Constitution
4.1. Success for the Republicans
4.2. Success for the Monarchists
5. The triumph of the Republicans.

---

***Answering essay questions on*** *'Uncertainties Resolved, 1871–9'*

The probability is that you will use evidence from this chapter mainly in answering essay questions of the general 'What threats?' and 'Why survive?' types. The discussion of these types of question is on pages 99–100.

But you may be asked to concentrate just on the years covered by the chapter. An example of such a question is,

'Why, between 1871 and 1879, did the French monarchists fail to achieve their aims?' (WJEC, 1980)

This is a straight-forward 'Why' question. You might like to construct an essay plan for it by going through the following stages:

1 Make a list of the statements that could be regarded as direct answers to this question. Begin each one with the word 'because', for example, 'because the monarchists were divided between Legitimists and Orleanists', and 'because the comte de Chambord would not compromise on the question of the *tricolore*'. There should be between five and eight statements in your list.
2 For each statement list the facts and evidence that you would need to include to substantiate your point.
3 Decide on an order of importance for your statements. Number them in descending order of importance.

---

*Source-based questions on 'Uncertainties Resolved, 1871–79'*

### 1 Chambord's Manifesto, July 1871
Read carefully Chambord's Manifesto, given on pages 28 and 29. Answer the following questions:
a)  What evidence does the Manifesto contain to suggest that Chambord was attempting to win the support of:
   i) those who opposed the highly centralized system of government that had existed in France since the time of Napoleon I;
   ii) those who opposed the way in which successive govenments had 'managed' elections so as to secure the return of their supporters;
   iii) the army?
b)  Why does Chambord regard the issue of the flag as a matter of honour?
c)  What does Chambord mean by 'the new barbarism that is menacing the world'? (line 59)
d)  For what reasons were Chambord's chief political supporters dismayed by this Manifesto?

### 2 The Political Crisis of 1877
Read carefully the extracts from Gambetta's letter (page 40), and MacMahon's letter (page 41).
Answer the following questions:
a)  Which of Gambetta's four possibilities does MacMahon's letter show actually happened?
b)  Why does Gambetta consider that the second of the possibilities he

lists is unlikely to happen?

c)  What assumptions does Gambetta make about the results of the election of 14 October? Give reasons for your answer.

d)  What are the implications of the words in brackets (lines 26–28) in MacMahon's letter?

e)  What action does MacMahon describe having taken following the election results?

f)  It could be argued that MacMahon's letter is conciliatory in tone. What evidence is there to support this view?

# CHAPTER 4

# Consolidation and Challenge, 1879–89

## 1 The Pattern of Politics

Jules Grévy, the third President of the Third Republic and the first to be elected by a majority of Republicans, was able to perform one great service to his country. He could convince the bourgeoisie and the conservative peasant farmers that a republican form of government did not necessarily bring in its wake revolution or even radical reform. This he was well suited by background and temperament to do. Although he had long been regarded as one of the leaders of the Republican cause, having made his mark in the heady days of 1848 and having remained loyal to his principles ever since, he was in fact very cautious. His Republicanism was based almost entirely on a wish to see a political system that invested all power in the freely elected representatives of the people. He did not wish to see extensive social reforms; if anything just the opposite. He was a great respecter of the rights of property and was likely to be hostile to any attempt to take from the rich and give to the poor, or to plans to remove effective economic and social power from the large landowners, industrialists, traders, bankers and professional men in order to give it to the peasantry or the workers.

His moderate views were shared by a majority of the Deputies who had been elected in 1877. In the 1881 election the trend was confirmed, and the resulting Chamber of Deputies contained a majority of men who wished to see change coming very slowly indeed. When Grévy came to power the leading Republican politician was Leon Gambetta, the man who had organized the national resistance to the advancing Prussian armies after the collapse of the Second Empire in September 1870, and it might have been expected that, once a Republican occupied the Presidency, he would be called upon to form a ministry. But this did not happen, for although Gambetta was the best known and most popular of the Republican leaders, he was greatly distrusted by many of his political colleagues. They remembered that he had made his reputation as a radical opponent of the former regime, and especially through his Belleville Programme, named after the working-class district of Paris where he announced his plans in 1869, which advocated major social reforms in the interests of the poor at the cost of the rich. They also resented his style of leadership which was largely based on the assumption that leaders lead and make decisions while followers follow and obey. This was not to the taste of the typical Republican Deputy, who was used to being a leader in his own locality and whose political power sprang from his own social and economic prominence in his community, not from the support of some national figure. They wanted to be led by men who would treat them as equals and who would be receptive to their demands for government measures that would be in the interests of their constituents. They therefore wished to see ministers who were relatively weak and amenable to pressure and who could be relied upon to pursue a policy that was generally aimed at maintaining the status quo. And this is how the Third Republic developed once the issue of the restoration of the monarchy was essentially buried with the resignation of MacMahon in 1879.

Grévy lost no time in assuring the country that he had no intention of acting in the manner of his predecessor. In his first speech as President he made it clear that he would not seek to use his power of asking the Senate to dissolve the Chamber of Deputies and to call for new elections. This, he said, would be undemocratic, for it would be an attempt to interfere with the voters' rights to be represented by whom they wished. In this his motives were pure because he had long argued that power should lie in the hands of the legislature (the elected representatives of the people) and not in the hands of the executive (the head of state, whether called King, Emperor or President). But the effects of his decision were far from those intended. Deputies were now assured that whatever they did they would be safe from the threat of facing a new election until the four-year life of the Assembly was at an end. They could therefore vote to bring down the Government whenever they wished because the only result would be that a new ministry would need to be formed.

 * If there had been well-developed political parties able to impose discipline on their members in the Chamber, or if the executive had been responsible for deciding the general trend of government policy, the situation would not have been serious. But parties as such did not really exist. There were many groupings that came into being for particular purposes, especially elections, but they were usually short-lived. Each of the major political figures was surrounded by a small group of supporters, often younger men who were prepared to fill the role of disciple, but they were not numerous enough to significantly effect the voting pattern in the Chamber. It is true that there was a clear division between the forces of the Right – Deputies who wished to see the restoration of the monarchy in one form or another – and those of the Left – Republicans who wished to see a continuation of the present regime. But there was little discipline within these broad groupings and it was not unusual to find elements of the Left and the Right voting together on particular issues. The Republicans tended to unite when they saw themselves under threat but this was rare. Much more common was the seemingly chaotic situation in which individual Deputies supported or deserted a ministry for purely personal or local reasons. Even the two broad groupings within the Republican movement, the Opportunists and the Radicals, did not vote together with any consistency. Research, using computers to analyse voting patterns, has shown that the politics of whim and fancy was a reality.

Nor could the President step in to rectify the situation and provide much needed continuity, for his role was now seen to be largely ceremonial. He could influence affairs by refusing to invite particular politicians to form a ministry, as long as the majority in the Chamber was prepared to accept somebody else, but he could not seek for people to implement 'his' policies, for it was assumed that it was not appropriate for the President to have such things. In practice, Grévy actually made the situation worse because he came into office determined not to have Gambetta as a minister, for he regarded him as a dangerous revolutionary, despite the fact that he had mellowed considerably since the days of his Belleville Programme. In this he was in effect colluding with the large number of Deputies who wished to ensure that ministries were led by men who were clearly open to influence.

So a pattern was established whereby effective power resided with the whole body of the Chamber of Deputies which, for the six months of each year it was in session, decided detailed matters of policy, often against the wishes of the ministers concerned. Ministries came and went with almost monotonous regularity, and it was unusual for one to survive for 12 months or more. Some continuity was provided by the fact that when a ministry fell it was normal for a majority of the ministers to be reappointed under a new Prime Minister, but this hardly contributed additional strength to the government for even such reappointed ministers had to continue to show themselves responsive to the wishes of the Chamber. As is normal in such situations, the ministries that tended to last longest were those that offended fewest people. This they did by remaining largely inactive. Those ministries that attempted great things were unlikely to continue in existence for many months.

In 1881 Grévy at last relented and accepted that Gambetta's position as the leading Republican figure meant that he should be invited to form a ministry. For those who were already disillusioned by the petty politicking that had seemed to become almost an end in itself, the news was greeted with great joy. Now it appeared that something constructive would at last be done. But it did not happen. Instead of Gambetta being able to unite the forces of Republicanism, he drove them further apart, for both those who feared change and those who wished for radical reform opposed his attempts to strike a middle course. After less than three months in power Gambetta was forced to resign. The Chamber of Deputies had shown, and had been seen to show, that it would not accept strong leadership in the normal course of events. Gambetta did not have long to come to terms with this state of affairs. In the next year he died at the age of 42. France had lost the one man of his generation who had the stature to unify the country in time of crisis. She was to feel the lack of him in years to come.

## 2 Jules Ferry

There was, however, one other Republican leader who, if he stood little chance of unifying the country, did possess the skills necessary to walk the tightrope of managing the Chamber while at the same time pursuing active policies. This was Jules Ferry. For much of the time between 1879 and 1885 he was in office either as Minister of Public Instruction (education minister) or as Prime Minister, and his record of achievement is impressive. It is true that he steered clear of those issues that could be seen as class issues, such as the restructuring of the taxation system in the interests of the poor that Gambetta had highlighted in his Belleville Programme, and concentrated on matters that, although highly contentious, could expect to be enthusiastically supported by elements of each class in society. But he showed himself to have a clear sense of purpose and was responsible, in totality or in part, for implementing policies that were to have far-reaching effects.

## a) Education Reforms

Ferry is perhaps most famous for his reforms affecting education. The issue he felt most strongly about, and the one he took most action over, was the question of the extent of the Catholic Church's control over the educational system. For centuries before the Revolution of 1789 what education had existed had been firmly in the hands of the Church authorities. Under Napoleon I the State had begun to take a major interest in the supply and control of schools and higher education, and in the years since 1815 one of the continuing controversies had been over the balance of power between the Church and the State in educational matters. Until 1870, the Church had been successful in maintaining the dominant position it had re-established during the Bourbon Restoration. Although it had lost the power to stipulate what should be taught and by whom, it was still the provider of schooling for nearly half of French children, even taking into account the minority who received no formal education.

Most of the schools run by the Church were staffed by monks and nuns, members of a wide variety of teaching orders, many of which had no legal status in France. They were allowed to operate outside the law because the authorities, both under Napoleon III and during the early conservative years of the Third Republic, had been prepared to turn a blind-eye to their activities. To convinced Republicans this situation was anathema. They could see the minds of the coming generation being moulded in the ways of religion and they knew that organized religion was hostile to Republicanism. They were especially opposed to the work of the Jesuits who, since their foundation in the sixteenth century, had proved themselves to be most effective in winning the hearts and minds of leading members of society to the Catholic cause. It was widely believed in anti-clerical circles that the Jesuits' success sprang from their use of methods that today would be called brainwashing, and there was a determination that they should not be allowed to continue their work in

France.

What most Republicans wanted was a state system of education under which every child would attend school freely and would be taught by properly trained teachers, which many of the monks and nuns were not, in schools where religion was not to form a part of the curriculum. Their hope was that all the teachers trained and employed by the State would be convinced republicans who would endeavour to pass on their political beliefs to the children they taught. Neither the Church nor the Republicans talked about neutrality in education: they both realized what a vital part schooling could play in ensuring them support in the future.

Ferry's attempt was to bring about laicity, the control of education by laymen rather than by churchmen. In order to do this he had to remove clerical influence from the state-run organizations controlling the educational system, and he had to reduce the numbers of children being taught in Church schools. Both he managed to achieve. Churchmen were removed from positions in which they could supervise state schools, and the granting of degrees and teaching qualifications was restricted to the state. More dramatically, and certainly with much more publicity, the Jesuits were expelled from France, along with the members of some less well-known teaching orders. But Ferry stopped short of closing the majority of Church schools, for had he done so, it would have been impossible to find the number of teachers required. So the influence of religious orders in education, although reduced, remained considerable.

As a compromise he concentrated on ensuring that the state system could offer proper competition by making primary education in state schools free, a lead that it was difficult for the Church schools to follow. At the same time, 1881-2, primary education was made compulsory for all. As a result, increasing numbers of children were educated by the State, in schools at which the teaching of religion was banned and by teachers who regarded themselves as propagandists for the regime. The balance of power in educational matters had significantly shifted, and this was to have a more and more marked effect as the years passed and as increasing numbers of citizens grew up having little or no contact with religion. More important at the time was the indication that the Republic was prepared to act against the interests of the Catholic Church. This strengthened the tendency of Catholics to regard the Republic as their enemy, and for them to line up with the forces of the Right in wishing to see a change of regime. This tendency was to feature strongly when the Republic came increasingly under attack during the last 15 years of the century.

## b) Political Reforms

When the constitutional arrangements had been drawn up by MacMahon and his friends on the Right in 1875, efforts had been made to restrict the 'pure' democracy advocated by radical Republicans. Little by little,

Ferry and the other leading Republicans dismantled what had been done. Their major complaint was against the Senate which they regarded as an unnecessary institution, set up merely to frustrate the will of the people. They would have liked to get rid of it altogether, but this was too extreme a course of action to win majority support in political circles. So instead, they satisfied themselves by making it less unrepresentative. It was agreed that no further life members would be appointed and that as existing life members died, their seats would be given to the more populous parts of the country that were currently very under-represented. There was also an improvement made in the way electoral colleges, which selected Senators, were composed. The current system was for each commune irrespective of size to have equal representation, which gave the countryside great power at the expense of the towns. In future large centres of population were given more votes, although, as the reformers were forced to compromise in order to gain majority support, this was not as many as their size would have warranted. Thus two of the abuses that had been built into the Senate were removed or reduced.

There was also a desire among 'advanced' Republicans to see a reduction in the degree of central control of local matters exercised by the government through the impressive administrative machinery orginally established by Napoleon I. Working through Prefects in each *département*, and through them down to Mayors in every Commune, control could be exercised in great detail. As all these officials were appointed and none were elected, it was seen by many people to be a system that was out of sympathy with Republican principles. Some would have liked to do away with the structure altogether but they were in a minority, for it was seen to have very real uses in ensuring efficient government in the localities. As a compromise measure the post of mayor was changed from appointive to elective in all areas except Paris, which was felt not to be ready for popular control so soon after the Commune. This was a considerable innovation because even Mayors were important agents of the national government, and to entrust official business to locally elected people seemed to many to be a dangerous departure from tradition. In practice, however, the new system worked well, with the local mayor, allied with the schoolmaster, being a powerful advocate and defender of the Republic.

Although elections to the Chamber of Deputies were by universal manhood suffrage, a system that was much in advance of most of Europe at the time, leading Republicans were discontented with the way in which elections were arranged. The traditional system of conducting elections (*scrutin de liste*) had been replaced by *scrutin d'arrondissement* in 1875 (see page 38). This was seen to favour candidates with strong local influence and was thought by republican leaders to inhibit the growth of proper parties, which it was felt would be encouraged if long lists of candidates for each *département* had to be produced. It was one of Ferry's successes that *scrutin d'arrondissement* was replaced by *scrutin de liste* in time for the 1885 elections.

Although the reforms that attracted most attention between 1881 and 1885 were those that affected the Senate, the election of mayors and the system of electing deputies for the Chamber, a number of other reforms were passed that showed the Republicans making sensible and necessary changes, even if not at the rate demanded by their radical colleagues. Freedom of the press was finally established, trade unions were legalized, and divorce was allowed. Recruitment to important parts of the civil service was carried out by competitive examination rather than by patronage. All magistrates who were known to be unsympathetic to the Republic were removed and replaced by supporters of the regime. It was even agreed that the heads of all former ruling families should be sent into exile, and that no members of their families should be allowed to hold positions in the armed services or be elected President. Thus the possibility of a restoration of the monarchy or Empire through a back door was finally ended. The plans of the founders of the Republic were now certain to come to nothing.

## c) Imperial Policy

All these achievements of Ferry and the Republicans were very much in line with what might have been expected from people holding their political views. What was surprising was the way in which Ferry was responsible for building up the French Empire overseas. Although in the years after the Revolution of 1789 Republicans had been in favour of territorial expansion, mainly to bring the benefits of liberty, equality and fraternity to people in neighbouring states, during the Second Empire a tradition had become established among them of deprecating foreign exploits. These were viewed as being wasteful and a distraction from domestic issues, as well as infringing the rights of other peoples to independence. Yet, due to the personal intervention of Ferry, the period up to 1885 saw the foundations laid of a new and extensive empire abroad. Ferry claimed that he was acting for economic reasons, wishing to secure for France sources of raw materials and potential markets for manufactured goods at a time when the growth of tariff barriers was endangering the continuation of the pattern of international trade as it was then known. He argued this case in the preface he wrote to a book in 1890.

1 . . . COLONIAL POLICY is the daughter of industrial policy. For wealthy States, where capital abounds and accumulates rapidly, where the manufacturing element is growing continuously, attracting the most energetic and restless if not the
5 most numerous section of that part of the population which lives by manual labour – where cultivation of the soil itself is forced to become mechanized in order to survive – exports are an essential factor of public prosperity. The spread of capital, like the demand

for work, is measured by the extent of the foreign market. If
10 manufacturing nations had been able to arrange a division of
industrial labour, a systematic and rational allocation of industry
according to the aptitudes, economics, natural, and social conditions of the different producer countries, setting the cotton
industry here, metallurgy there, reserving alcohols and sugars for
15 one, woollens and silks for the other, Europe might not have
needed markets for its products beyond its own boundaries. But
nowadays everybody wants to spin and weave, forge and distil. All
Europe refines far too much sugar and wants to export it. The
United States on one hand, and Germany on the other, have
20 entered the stage as the last-comers to manufacturing industry.
The starting of an industrial era in all its forms for the little states,
from peoples who were dominant or exhausted, for Italy regener-
ated, for Spain enriched by French capital, for the Swiss who are so
enterprising and so shrewd, all these factors have placed
25 the whole of the West, except so far Russia, who is growing and
nearly ready, on a slope which we shall not ascend again.

On the other side of the Vosges and across the Atlantic the
protective-tariff system has increased manufactures, closed former
outlets and introduced strong competition into the European
30 market. Defending oneself by raising barriers in return is some
help, but not enough. . . .

The protective system is like a steam engine without a safety
valve if it has no healthy, genuine colonial policy as a corrective and
auxiliary. The plethora of capital invested in industry tends not
35 only to diminish the profits from capital, but to halt the rise in
wages, which is nevertheless the natural beneficent law of modern
societies. Nor is it an abstract law, but a being compounded of flesh
and bone, passion and will, which moves, complains and defends
itself. In the industrial age of humanity, social peace is a question of
outlets. . . . The European consumer market is saturated. New
40 layers of consumers must be brought in from other parts of the
globe. If this is not done, modern society will go bankrupt, and
as the twentieth century dawns, social liquidation will have been
prepared by way of cataclysm with incalculable consequences.
45   It is because England was the first to perceive those distant
horizons that she has headed the modern industrial movement. It is
because of possible setbacks which her industrial hegemony could
suffer through the detachment of Australia and India, after the
separation of the United States from North America, that she is
50 laying siege to Africa on four fronts: on the south, through the Cape
plateau and Bechuanaland; on the west through the Niger and the
Congo; on the northeast, through the valley of the Nile; and on the
east through Suakin, the Somali coast, and the basin of the great
equatorial lakes. In order to prevent British enterprise from

55  capturing for its exclusive profit the new markets that are opening
    up for western products, Germany is opposing England at all
    points of the globe with a rivalry which is as inconvenient as it was
    unexpected. Colonial policy is an international manifestation of the
    eternal laws of competition. . . .

It seems, however, that there must have been other reasons, for the
economic argument failed to convince many people at the time or later. It
seems likely, although it can never be known for certain, that Ferry
wished to increase France's prestige and international standing, and that
he could find no other way of doing it. Certainly he was convinced that
the widespread demand for *revanche* against Germany, and a war to
recover Alsace and Lorraine, were totally unrealistic and that, if pursued, would result in certain defeat and disgrace. But Bismarck was
prepared to encourage France's colonial aspirations, both in order to
distract her from the Rhine and in the hope that expansion overseas
would bring her into conflict with her potential allies, especially Britain
and Italy, in any future war against Germany. In this he was successful,
although not always in the way he had expected.
    In 1881 Ferry managed to engineer the establishment of a protectorate
over Tunisia. In the years since Charles X's expedition against Algiers in
1830, huge amounts of money and large numbers of lives had been
expended on extending and securing France's hold on Algeria. In order
to gain the neighbouring territory to the east, which, it was feared, Italy
was about to annex, Ferry grossly exaggerated the scope of raids into
Algeria from across the border with Tunisia and managed to secure the
Chamber's approval of a retaliatory expedition. When this speedily
resulted in 1881 in a draft treaty with the Bey of Tunisia (the ruler of the
area) in which he sought France's protection, the Chamber had little
choice but to accept what was really a *fait accompli*. But many Deputies
did not like the way in which their hands had been forced and were
alerted against falling into the same trap again.
    When in 1882 the next opportunity came to strengthen France's hold in
North Africa, Ferry was out of office. Civil disturbances in Egypt were
threatening the rule of law and order and the security of the vitally
important Suez Canal was thought to be in danger. Recognizing France's
historic links with Egypt, which had been strong since Napoleon had
invaded it in the 1790s, Britain invited the French government to engage
in joint action to restore stability to the country. The offer was hesitat-
ingly accepted, but once the action needed to be extended beyond the
sending of a fleet to look threatening, the Chamber was not prepared to
support a bombardment or a landing of troops. So Britain was left to
intervene on her own, and just as in 1881 France had declared a protecto-
rate over Tunisia, Britain did so in Egypt a year later. Although this
caused little upset in France to begin with, it was soon seen to be a huge
mistake. Britain had been allowed to establish control of a key strategic

area which was clearly in France's 'zone of influence'. As often happens when there is a need to cover up a mistake, great blame was heaped on Britain for supposed duplicity. Egypt never loomed as large as Alsace–Lorraine in the French consciousness, but it occupied a good second place and for 20 years gave good reason to resurrect the traditional dislike of the neighbours across the Channel.

Between 1883 and 1885 Ferry was Prime Minister for a second time. He pressed ahead vigorously with the securing of new colonies and the extension of existing ones. This was despite the continual attacks from the Right who disliked his colonial policy as necessitating a reliance on Bismarck's support, whereas they thought France should be preparing to fight him, and the Radicals who objected to large amounts of money being spent in this way. The French hold on Madagascar, a very large island off the east coast of Africa, was strengthened, and when the interested powers met in Berlin in 1884 to decide what should happen to the Congo Basin in Central Africa, France emerged with a huge new colony, later known as the French Congo. But still large numbers of Republican Deputies were not convinced that this type of forward policy was in France's best interests. Napoleon III's calamitous attempt to establish an empire in Mexico was too recent a memory, and many people predicted that Ferry was leading the country into unwanted entanglements and towards disaster. When news came from Indo-China that the attempt to spread French control northwards was being met with stout Chinese resistance and had resulted in military reverses that would require considerable reinforcements to put right, a majority was at last found in the Chamber which was prepared to bring down Ferry's government. Yet, although the politicians who attacked Ferry so visciously were not prepared to initiate new ventures, they were unwilling to see previous efforts wasted and the new government quietly consolidated the position that had been established in Indo-China. There was clearly an element of hypocrisy in the attacks they made on Ferry, even though they thought it would have been preferable for his initiatives not to have been taken in the first place.

## 3 General Boulanger

The result of the election of 1885 was something of a shock to the Republicans. When, in the 1881 election, the vote for candidates of the Right had diminished considerably, it had been assumed that the future lay with the supporters of the regime. And now that *scrutin d'arrondissement* had been replaced by *scrutin de liste* (see page 38), it was hoped that there would be greater party discipline among the Republicans, resulting in stronger and longer lasting governments. But their hopes were dashed when the Right made a spectacular recovery and secured enough seats to deny the Opportunists the majority they had enjoyed between 1881 and 1885, and when the efforts to build a proper Republican party machine in order to draw up the departmental lists of candidates came to nothing in the face of a multitude of local groupings which were unprepared to give way to central direction. So instead of 1885 marking the coming of age of the Republic, it brought a set-back and greater instability, as the large grouping of moderate Republicans, the Opportunists, had now to woo either the left-wing Republicans, the Radicals, or sections of the Right in order to secure a majority for any government they put forward. To make matters worse, the Opportunists could not be relied upon to act with any great sense of group loyalty or solidarity. So the pattern of relatively weak and short-lived governments continued.

As part of a deal done by the Opportunists with Georges Clemenceau, the leading figure among the Radicals, General Boulanger was appointed Minister of War in January 1886. In normal circumstances and with a run-of-the-mill soldier this would have been of no great significance. But unbeknown to Clemenceau, who thought he was merely sponsoring an up and coming man who wished to implement reforms of the army that were in line with the views of radical Republicans, a train of events was being started that was to put the Republic in great danger and was to make many people think that its days were numbered.

Georges Boulanger was the youngest of the army's generals when he was appointed Minister of War at the age of 48. A man of great ambition, he had been fortunate to gain rapid promotion during the war with Prussia. He possessed the social graces needed to win the support of the important people who could ensure his further progress towards the top. He impressed both by the way he looked and by the way he acted. He was regarded as being particularly handsome in a way that was unusual for Frenchmen: he had blue eyes and a blond beard. His bearing was that of a man to whom authority came naturally, but he was also charming and considerate in a way that allowed people of both sexes and of differing political views to think of him as a fine man rather than as a man who was challenging them. A hundred years later he might have starred in a popular television series.

## a) In Office

He quickly made his mark as a public figure once he was in office. He took immediate action to implement the army reforms he had previously advocated, especially those that made the lives of ordinary soldiers more tolerable, such as the detailed arrangements for their feeding and accommodation. These reforms brought him rapid popularity. He even laid plans to put into effect two of the major policies of the Radicals: the shortening of the term of service in the army to three years, and the ending of the system by which privileged groups could avoid military service altogether. He appealed to the widespread anti-clerical feeling in the country by insisting that priests must in future serve their time along with everyone else. But these were not the main causes of the wave of

*General Boulanger, 14 July 1886*

hero worship that quickly spread across the country. It was the romantic and dashing image of the man rather than anything particular he did which caused the crowds to cheer him and which led to a spate of music-hall songs about him as others rushed to cash in on the new idol of the day. In a time before records and videos he was filling the public's need to have a super-star to envy and adore.

By the time of the military parade on 14 July, France's National Day, public support for Boulanger was so great that the events that took place seemed to centre on him rather than on Jules Grévy, the President. Even at this stage there were many politicians who were beginning to wonder where it would end, for already there were clear parallels with the events that had led up to Louis Napoleon's *coup* 35 years earlier. But it was to take a little more time for a majority in the Chamber to see the danger, and Boulanger retained his position when a new ministry was formed in the following December.

By the Spring of 1887 more suspicions had been aroused. Using a petty border incident in which an organizer of French agents in Alsace-Lorraine had been arrested by the Germans, Boulanger responded to strong popular feeling by making ominous noises about a possible war. His reputation was greatly enhanced when Bismarck both attacked him by name as a warmonger and arranged the release of the captive official. It seemed to many ordinary French people that here at last was a leader of whom the Germans were afraid and who could be relied upon to guide the nation to greatness and revenge. But to the majority of Republican politicians who were aware of France's military limitations and were determined not to allow one of their number to become too powerful, the moment was right to cut the General down to size. As there was no pretext that could be used to demand his resignation, it was necessary for the whole ministry to be defeated and replaced by one in which Boulanger would not be invited to serve. This happened in May 1887, but it did nothing to reduce the popularity of the man who was increasingly being seen as the new Napoleon.

## b) Biding his Time

Boulanger out of office was if anything more dangerous than Boulanger in office, for now he had ample opportunity to make the public appearances that fuelled the flame of his popularity. It was clear to the authorities that if he were allowed to appear in a second 14 July parade a situation would be created in which a *coup* just might be possible. It seemed that the army, although not prepared to seize power for itself, was unlikely to come to the rescue of a regime that was proving itself incapable of providing the strong leadership necessary for *revanche* to be achieved. If Boulanger and his supporters were to take over the key buildings in Paris with the assent of a large number of local citizens, there would be no way in which they could be removed, and the Third

Republic would crumble in the same way as had the Second Empire 17 years previously.

The government decided to force the issue at a time of its choosing rather than waiting for events to take their natural course: Boulanger was ordered to take up a command in a remote area of the south, reporting for duty a week before the 14 July parade. Yet he was allowed to make the most of the situation, for he was not prevented from travelling by public transport and from announcing the train on which he would be travelling. Huge crowds appeared at the station determined to prevent his departure. Large numbers of people even lay down on the rails to prevent the train from moving. But the authorities were not prepared to surrender the initiative totally, and Boulanger was whisked to an alternative platform where a second train was waiting to speed him on his way. It appeared that the crisis was over. Boulanger conducted himself properly, carrying out the duties that were assigned to him, and once he was removed from the public eye his popularity dwindled in the heat of the summer. The politicians hoped that things could now return to normal. But it was not to be.

In October 1887 a scandal emerged that went right to the heart of Republican institutions. Daniel Wilson, the son-in-law of the President, was accused of using family connections to sell political honours. To make matters worse, he was a Deputy of high standing himself and not only lived as a guest in the presidential palace, but also used the President's free postal service to conduct his extensive private business. There was no doubt in the public's mind that Wilson was guilty and even hardened politicians could see that the President, Jules Grévy, would have to resign as a result of his son-in-law's dishonesty. But Grévy did not agree, and the country was treated to the unedifying spectacle of the Government resigning in order to force the President out, and the President only going once all the leading politicians in turn had refused to form a new ministry. The more cynical commentators explained the long drawn-out crisis in terms of Grévy's desire to remain in office until 1 December and thus to draw an additional month's salary. Grévy was known to be extremely mean, even miserly, and to have built up large savings from refusing to spend the bulk of his presidential salary, so it is possible that he did hold out for a day or two longer than he otherwise would have done.

In France politicians had always been treated with less respect than in Britain, for instance, and the Wilson Affair gave yet further proof that parliamentarians and parliamentary institutions were not really to be trusted, as Monarchists and other members of the Right had long contended. Coming at a time when the Third Republic had been in existence for 17 years, which was about the lifetime of the longer lasting regimes since 1789, and when Boulanger seemed to have the potential of being a viable alternative, it is not surprising that many people thought that the regime was nearing its end.

This impression was strengthened by the way in which a successor to Grévy was selected. Many Opportunists would have been happy to see Ferry, their effective leader, elected to office. But there were enough who, in combination with the Right and the Radicals, wanted to see a relatively weak man as President to ensure that Ferry was not elected. After much searching and back-room bargaining, a generally acceptable candidate was found. He was Sadi Carnot, whose only personal claim to fame was his brilliance as an engineer, but who had the good fortune to be the grandson of one of the great Republican figures of the 1790s and the son of one of the stalwarts of the Republican establishment. He was a dull and well-meaning man who was seen to have been chosen because of his expected mediocrity. It is illuminating that the apocryphal story circulated that Clemenceau's instruction to his followers was 'to vote for the stupidest'. This seemed to typify the level to which politics in the Republic had sunk. The time was clearly right for Boulanger to emerge from the obscurity of the south.

## c) Challenge for Power

The months since July 1887 had not been wasted. The Republican politicians might have thought that the crisis was over once the train carrying the General left Paris, but the enemies of the regime could see that Boulanger was far from finished. It was true that for most people it was 'out of sight out of mind', but he was not in the least discredited. He still had the ability to be all things to all people. The warlike attitude he had adopted towards Germany made the Right feel that here might be a man to fulfil their ambitions. And they were looking for a figurehead, for the Legitimists no longer had a candidate for power since Chambord's death in 1884, while the death of the Prince Imperial in 1879 had left the Bonapartists without an acceptable leader. In theory, the Orleanist claimant, the comte de Paris, should have been the focus of attention for the Right, but he was a somewhat colourless character whose avowed support of a parliamentary form of government made him an unattractive proposition as it was just this feature of the Third Republic that made many people despair.

Strangely enough, for a man who had entered politics as a radical Republican, Boulanger was more than prepared to listen to the overtures of the Right. Perhaps it was because Monarchists provided a ready source of funds to mount a major campaign, or because he was disillusioned by the treatment he had received from the Republicans, or even because he was a man of no principles who was prepared to follow whichever course seemed most expedient at the time. For whatever reason, and it was most likely a mixture of all three, Boulanger made his plans with elements of the Right. It was decided that he would stand in each by-election that occurred, resigning each time he was successful so that he would be free to be a candidate the next time. His policy would be anti-parliamentarian, demanding the dissolution of the present Chamber and its replacement by a Constituent Assembly that would be empowered to draw up a new Constitution aimed at providing stronger leadership from the top. It was naturally hoped that this new strong leadership would be provided by Boulanger.

This was a clever plan because each by-election under the system of *scrutin de liste* took place across a whole *département* giving maximum publicity and allowing Boulanger's supporters to claim that each contest was a mini-plebiscite. To the government's horror he won six of the seven by-elections held in 1888, and in the process built up public excitement almost to fever pitch. The climax came in January 1889 when the first seat to fall vacant in Paris came to be filled. Both sides were of the opinion that here was a make or break contest and huge sums of money were spent on publicity. Boulanger's address to the electors was a cleverly calculated mixture of defence and attack.

1 ELECTORS OF THE SEINE,

The parliamentarians, who have done all they could to prevent my standing for election, are panic-stricken today at the idea of seeing me elected. My sword upset them. They took it away from
5 me. And now they are more anxious than when I was still wearing it.

In reality, it is not me they are frightened of, but universal suffrage, whose repeated decisions testify to the disgust the country feels at the state of degeneracy to which their incapacity,
10 low intrigues, and tedious debates have brought the Republic.

It is in fact more convenient to make me responsible for the discredit into which they have fallen than to attribute it to their egoism and their indifference to the interest and sufferings of the people.
15 In order not to be forced to accuse themselves, they accuse me, by alleging that I have the most unlikely dictatorial plans. For they dismissed me as minister on the pretext that I was for war, and they attack me as a candidate on the pretext that I am for dictatorship.

Dictatorship! Were we not subjected to it in all its forms? Does a
20 day pass without some proposal to invent exceptional laws for our electors and for me?

If the thought of playing at being dictator had occurred to me, I think it would have done so when, as Minister for War, I had the whole army in my grasp. Did anything in my attitude then justify
25 this insulting suspicion? No! I accepted the sympathy of all without thinking of touting for popularity from anybody. What is there dictatorial in a programme which advocates constitutional revision by the most democratic system, by means of a Constituent Assembly, where each deputy will have every opportunity to
30 defend and win acceptance for his opinions?

The leaders of the Republican Party had relied upon my Republicanism when they opened the doors of the ministry to me. Give me one single act, one single profession of faith, in which I have not clearly pledged my word.

35   But I want, and France wants, a Republic composed of something other than a collection of ambitions and greed.

What can we hope from men who, on their own admission, have deceived you for fifteen years, and now dare to present themselves to you and ask once more for your confidence?

40   Electors of the Seine,
France today is eager for justice, rectitude, and unselfishness.

I want to serve her once more by trying, with you, to cut out the wastage which is exhausting her and the rivalries that degrade her.

*La Patrie* is our patrimony, for all of us. You will prevent it from
45 becoming the prey of a few.
Long live France!
Long live the Republic!

General Boulanger

The result was amazing. Boulanger swept to victory by winning the votes of most of the radical Republicans as well as those of the traditional Right. It was widely expected – and accepted – that this triumph would be immediately followed by a fairly bloodless *coup* after which Boulanger would put his policies into effect. But it did not happen.

* The Government could hardly believe its good fortune, but as the days and weeks passed and nothing more than rowdy celebrations took place, the Republicans realized that they had a real chance of survival. They decided to go on to the offensive. They let it be known that plans were being made to arrest Boulanger on charges of attempting to subvert the State. The plan worked and in April the now ex-General – he had been dismissed from the army for indiscipline during the by-election campaign – fled to Belgium and, despite the entreaties of his leading supporters, refused to return. The bubble had burst. The Boulangists still managed to win 40 seats in the general election held in the autumn of 1889 but the crisis was over. The Republic had survived.

Many explanations have been given for the way in which Boulanger failed when it would have been easier to succeed. They all revolve around the personality of the man, which clearly had some flaws as far as being a successful revolutionary was concerned. Besides being an inveterate and transparent liar, which led to him confusing even himself at times, he was a man of ambition but no conviction. There was nothing he really wanted to do with power if he attained it; he was more interested in being important and having a good time. So he was not prepared to risk his happiness in an attempt to overthrow the regime, which if unsuccessful would have resulted in imprisonment and even death. He would have assumed power if the Republic had crumbled before him, but he was not prepared to overthrow it himself. By the time of the Paris by-election he was, in fact, so much in love with his mistress of the moment that he had no stronger desire than to enjoy her company for the rest of his life. He preferred her to the prospect of supreme power in France and to this decision he remained constant. If he had not lost so much public sympathy by deserting his millions of followers in order to pursue his private life, his end would seem tragic. After two years of blissful life together his mistress died, and Boulanger, grief-stricken beyond endurance, shot himself on her grave. Like much of his life there was something very theatrical about his death, but at least he had proved that he did not lack courage when he felt strongly enough about something.

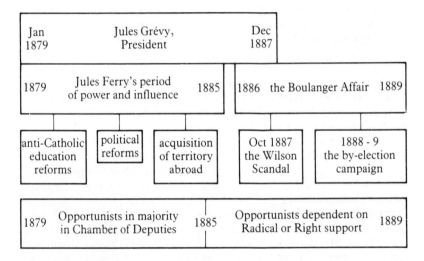

| Jan 1879 | Jules Grévy, President | | Dec 1887 | |
|---|---|---|---|---|
| 1879 | Jules Ferry's period of power and influence | 1885 | 1886   the Boulanger Affair   1889 | |
| anti-Catholic education reforms | political reforms | acquisition of territory abroad | Oct 1887 the Wilson Scandal | 1888 - 9 the by-election campaign |
| 1879   Opportunists in majority in Chamber of Deputies   1885 | | | Opportunists dependent on Radical or Right support   1889 | |

*Summary – Consolidation and Challenge, 1879–89*

**Making notes on *'Consolidation and Challenge, 1879–89'***

The three sections of this chapter deal with one 'situation' and two sets of 'events'. Your notes on each section should make it clear what was the state of affairs or what happened, while indicating, wherever possible, what were the causes and effects of what you are describing. Because it is only part of a broader topic, make your notes as brief as you can. Only include as much detail as is necessary to remind you of the pattern of events. The following headings and sub-headings should serve you well:

---

*Answering essay questions on 'Consolidation and Challenge, 1879–89'*

You will have plenty of opportunity to include information about Ferry and Boulanger in essays on the Third Republic, but you will probably never write an essay about either of them on their own.

They will feature in general questions about the whole period. There is an obvious need to include a consideration of the Boulanger affair in any discussion of the threats to the continued existence of the Third Republic. You might find it helpful to draw up a list of statements directly answering the question, 'In what ways did Boulanger pose a threat to the Third Republic?' For each statement indicate your opinion of the seriousness of the threat.

Both Ferry and Boulanger need to find a place in most 'Why survive?' questions. What points would you wish to include to support answering statements such as, 'because leading opponents of the regime after 1871 were unwilling or unable to act decisively at critical moments', and 'because sufficient reforms were passed to satisfy moderate supporters of the Left'?

Occasionally you might be faced by a question on a quite restricted span of time. The shorter period can be variable and can include events before and/or after those examined in this chapter. Three examples, moving from the quite specific to the fairly general, are:

'Was the Third French Republic in serious danger between 1875 and 1886?' (Cambridge, 1982)

'Account for the failure of French governments between 1875 and 1895 to achieve reconciliation between the conflicting forces in French society.' (Cambridge, 1981)

'How serious were the internal threats faced by the Third Republic in the first three decades of its existence?' (JMB, 1981)

With questions of this type, which specify a span of years within a more general period, it is essential to identify which of the issues/topics you have studied fall within the scope of the question and which do not. For instance, in which of the questions above would a consideration of the Boulanger Affair *not* be appropriate?

If you were constructing an essay plan in answer to the first question, what statements would you include to support a 'Yes' answer and what to support a 'No' answer? In what order would you present your points? Page 99 may help you in deciding this.

---

*Source-based questions on 'Consolidation and Challenge, 1879–89'*

### 1 Ferry's Colonial Policy

Read carefully the extract from Ferry's writings on pages 52–54. Answer the following questions:

a) What, according to Ferry, were the effects of the growth of international tariff barriers?

b) What argument does Ferry use in an attempt to frighten his readers into supporting a forward colonial policy?

c) What explanations could be given of the fact that France was not mentioned once in the extract?

d) Events since 1890 have proved Ferry wrong. What have been found to be the main flaws in his argument?

### 2 General Boulanger

Study carefully the picture of Boulanger on page 57, and his election address on pages 61 and 62.
Answer the following questions:

a) What events is Boulanger alluding to when he writes, 'My sword upset them. They took it away from me.' (line 4)?

b) What are the main elements of Boulanger's attack on the politicians in power at the time?

c) Boulanger attempts to discredit the arguments that his opponents are using against him. How successful is he in doing this?

d) The picture of Boulanger and the election address are different in tone. What is this difference? Give reasons for this difference.

# CHAPTER 5

# The Panama Scandal and the Dreyfus Affair

In the 1890s the Republic was rocked by two more affairs which at times were thought by some commentators to be likely to lead to the collapse of the regime. Unlike the Boulanger Affair, however, neither of the crises that followed was caused by people attempting to usurp power for themselves. Both resulted from the discovery that important people had acted improperly in their conduct of official business. The outcries that followed centred on charges of corruption and the perversion of justice. As each of the affairs lasted for years rather than for weeks or months, the enemies of the Third Republic were given ample opportunity to organize themselves so as to take advantage of the situation.

## 1 The Panama Scandal

The first crisis surrounded what has variously been called 'the Panama Affair' or 'the Panama Scandal'. Panama, that area of Central America where the land dividing the Atlantic and Pacific Oceans is at its narrowest, had for a long time attracted international attention, for if a canal could be built across it, huge savings of time and money would be made, as ships would no longer have to undertake the risky journey around South America in order to pass from one ocean to the other. But nobody had been found who was willing to attempt to construct such a canal. It was well known that it would be a very costly venture and one that would be uncertain of success because the terrain to be crossed was so difficult. In neither the USA, which was geographically best placed to take action, nor Britain, whose extensive world trade would make her one of the major beneficiaries of a canal at Panama, were there prominent people who considered that an attempt to construct a canal would represent a sensible financial investment.

In France the situation was different. In Ferdinand de Lesseps the international pressure group in favour of the construction of a Panama canal found a figure of national importance who was an enthusiastic supporter of the venture. Lesseps had made his name as the builder of the Suez Canal in the 1860s and was regarded in France as one of the few great men that the country possessed. He was a larger than life character whose charisma and colossal self-confidence led many ordinary people to have absolute faith in him. After all, he had brought great prestige to France by achieving at Suez what many had thought was impossible. When, in 1881, he launched a scheme to repeat the performance in Panama, there were tens of thousands of French people who were prepared to accept the great man's assurances that it could and would be done.

## a) The Panama Canal Company

Following the pattern he had set with Suez, Lesseps raised the capital required for his Panama Canal Company by selling shares to a multitude of small investors. This was not the normal way of raising large quantities of capital, which was usually done by negotiating loans from the large banks, but Lesseps believed in spreading the ownership of private-enterprise companies as widely as possible. Almost as a matter of principle, he wished to obtain his financial support from the ordinary people. He was successful, and relatively easily raised the money he thought was required. The early work on the site, however, soon showed that Lesseps had seriously underestimated the cost of construction. It was necessary to raise more money and in 1883 and 1884 this was done, although with some difficulty, despite the fact that he still felt able to promise that the canal would be opened in 1888.

At a similar stage in the building of the Suez Canal, when additional money had been required to assure completion, the device of a lottery loan had been used. Lottery loans were not unlike modern-day premium bonds in that the money loaned was not lost even if the investor was not one of the lucky people to win a large prize in the lottery. It was a scheme that attempted to capitalize on the gambling instincts of ordinary people. Unfortunately, as far as Lesseps was concerned, a lottery loan could only be arranged once Parliament had given its approval. This permission was sought in 1885 but it was not until 1888 that it was granted. In the meantime attempts to raise the urgently needed money by the further public sale of shares was becoming more and more difficult as most of those who wished to support the company had already invested as much as they wanted to. By the time the lottery loan was approved the Company was in serious financial difficulties, and the money raised by the new method was not enough to save it. In 1889 Lesseps declared the Panama Canal Company to be bankrupt and the receivers were called in. The first stage of the crisis had begun.

Thousands of ordinary Frenchmen, many of them peasants and shopkeepers, had lost everything they had invested, because it was immediately clear that little value could be gained from a partially completed canal. For many people it was a matter of carefully accumulated life savings having been lost. The news of the collapse was met at first with widespread incomprehension. There had been no sign that all was not going well, and it was only a matter of months since fresh loans had been raised. For many the shock was followed closely by considerable anger, and the feeling was widespread that 'they', whoever 'they' were, had been responsible for misleading the public about the reality of the situation. As 'they' was normally used to refer to all those in power and authority, faith in the 'system' by which the country was run was considerably shaken. Boulanger had argued that all was not well in the higher reaches of power and authority, and the failure of the Panama Canal Company seemed to confirm what he had claimed.

## b) Causes of Collapse

Yet the truth of the matter seems to be that arrogance and stupidity rather than corruption and deceit caused the collapse of Lesseps' scheme. Ferdinand de Lesseps was clearly a remarkable man, and although he was 75 when the Panama Canal Company was formed, he was still far from senility. But he was not, and never had been, a civil engineer. He was an effective entrepreneur and publicist whose technical knowledge was very limited. In the building of the Suez Canal he had ignored much of the technical advice he had been given, and had got away with it because by chance it proved possible to build the canal as he wanted it, not as his engineers said it would have to be.

Over Panama he was not so lucky. He wanted a canal at sea level which ships would be able to steam through without passing through complicated sets of locks. His advisers warned him that this would only be possible at a huge cost because of the high land in the middle of the isthmus. Lesseps decided that the deep cut would be made so that the canal would be at sea level throughout. By the time he listened to reason and changed his mind a considerable proportion of the Company's capital had been expended on work that should have been avoided.

Yet even without this mistake, the result of ignorance allied to stubborn pride, there would have been problems. Lesseps had dramatically underestimated the cost of the work that was necessary. Before the Company collapsed it had spent three times the amount originally planned and the task was far from complete. Although he had been properly briefed about it, he discounted the effect of the yellow fever that was rife in the area and which killed many of those sent to work on the construction of the canal, while it severely reduced the capacity of those who survived. Illness and death added considerably to the Company's expenses. So too did the high cost and ineffectiveness of local labour, both of which Lesseps had been warned about well in advance, but which he had chosen to discount as pessimism on the part of some of his advisers.

There can be little doubt that the Panama Canal Company failed largely because it was led by a man who mistakenly believed that will power rather than sound judgment was what was needed to make a success of major schemes of construction. Equally, there can be little doubt that Lessep's mistakes were honest mistakes. He was not corrupt. He suffered considerable financial loss with the Company's collapse, as well as sustaining a blow to his reputation that was keenly felt. More than anyone else, he had wanted his venture to be a success.

## c) The Scandal

It took two years for the receivers to work their way through the Company's accounts. During this time, and for some months afterwards, there was no suggestion that there had been any criminal activities involved in the failure of Lesseps' scheme. Then, in 1892, articles began to appear in the newspapers claiming that huge sums of money had been spent by the Company in bribing important people, including senior politicians. The campaign was led by Edouard Drumont, the editor of the *Libre Parole* newspaper, who had already established for himself a reputation as an extreme and violently worded anti-Semite. Drumont tried to prove that the Company had used Jewish financiers to buy the support of leading Republicans and to ensure the silence of those who knew that work at Panama was not progressing according to plan. His contention was that this was yet another example of the way in which the international Jewish financial fraternity was taking over effective control of the country by corrupting the key figures of the Republic. Hitler was to make similar claims in Germany in the 1920s and early 1930s. Although it was clear to all but Drumont's fellow extremists that the claim of an international plot to seize control of the State was ridiculous, there was enough substance in the detailed allegations to suggest that some illegalities had taken place.

What in fact seems to have happened was that Lesseps used a Jewish financier, Baron Jacques de Reinach, to undertake what today would be described as the public relations side of the business. As was quite normal when a company intended to raise money directly from the public, large sums were spent in creating a favourable image for the scheme. Newspaper owners, editors and journalists were paid to write or publish favourable articles, and the people who sold the Company's shares did so on very advantageous terms.

Less normal was what happened once the Company was safely launched but was in need of further capital. Newspaper people found that they could draw a regular income from the Company by agreeing not to allow any adverse publicity about Panama to appear, and members of parliament were able to ask for help with all sorts of expenses as long as they did nothing that was antagonistic to the Company. The situation became serious once attempts were made in 1885 to obtain permission to float the lottery loan. At least one minister asked for, and was paid, a large sum of money for his active support, and it seems likely that numbers of other Senators and Deputies were bribed to vote in favour of the proposal.

Exactly what happened will never be known because, for obvious reasons, accurate records of these dealings were not kept. Those that were kept were destroyed in mysterious circumstances and the major figures told so many lies that it has subsequently proved impossible to separate truth from falsehood with any certainty. The bad odour that surrounded the affair was worsened by the fact that Reinach worked partly through a disreputable Jewish businessman, Cornelius Herz, who was quite prepared to use blackmail as well as bribery. The full part that Herz played in the proceedings is unknown, but it is probable that he used blackmail to extort through Reinach huge sums of money, totalling nearly one per cent of the Company's assets.

As more and more allegations appeared in the press during 1892, the politicians who had received money from the Company became more and more uneasy. The unease was increased when, in November, Reinach died. It was claimed that he had committed suicide, fearing that his full part in the affair was about to be revealed. In December the parliamentary immunity of those politicians suspected of having been bribed was removed, and during 1893 the trials of Lesseps, his fellow directors and of a number of politicians were held. It turned out to be almost impossible to produce evidence that would secure conviction in a court of law. Lesseps was found guilty of fraud and was imprisoned, but the evidence was poor and he was rightly freed on appeal. One politician, the minister who had demanded money to support the lottery loan proposal, admitted his guilt and was sentenced to five years in prison. The rest were acquitted through lack of evidence.

* While the Panama Scandal was at its height in 1892 it seemed that great harm was being done to the regime by the revelation that leading members of the Republican group in parliament were probably corrupt. Some thought that the Third Republic was about to crumble. However, the enemies of the regime were in no fit state to take advantage of the situation as they were still recovering from the disappointment of Boulanger and had no person of stature to lead them, while the Republicans themselves were not sufficiently demoralized by the affair to relinquish power voluntarily. So the measurable effects of the Scandal were few. A number of quite prominent politicians disappeared from view either permanently or temporarily. One of these was Georges Clemenceau, the leading Radical, whose enemies used his close association with Cornelius Herz as a weapon with which to drive him from political life. But there was no suggestion that he had received money from the Company. In the general election of 1893 the Scandal did not feature widely and many of those who were suspected of having received bribes were safely returned. It seemed that the population as a whole was not interested in what had happened.

Yet those who would argue that the Panama Scandal is only important as providing an indication of the true nature of the Third Republic are misjudging the situation. Although it is impossible to prove, it seems very likely that the affair contributed significantly to the widespread feeling that parliamentary democracy was nothing more than a system by which influential people furthered their own interests. There was no great faith in politicians and the political process in France as it was. For many people it seems that Panama merely confirmed what they thought they already knew. The telling factor about the 1893 election was not that most of the suspected politicians were re-elected, but that 30 per cent of the electorate chose not to vote, a figure that was very high for France. The Panama Scandal was a further encouragement to those who believed that the only way forward lay in taking action outside of the normal political framework.

## 2 The Dreyfus Affair

Hardly had the events surrounding the failure of the Panama Canal Company taken their course than the newspapers were featuring another possible scandal. Somebody, it was claimed, was selling military secrets to the Germans. What followed was a series of events that divided France more dramatically than had anything since the Revolution of 1789.

Before the mid-nineteenth century the concept of military secrets in peacetime hardly existed. The development of increasingly sophisticated weapons, complex defensive fortifications, and detailed plans for the movement and deployment of troops if war threatened made it increasingly important to know how potential enemies would be armed, defended and deployed in time of war. So all the European Powers developed methods of finding out about each other's military preparations. As it was thought not to be quite 'gentlemanly' to employ permanent spies, the normal way was to buy information from free-lance spies who were recognized as having no loyalties and being prepared to spy on anybody and to sell to anybody. By the 1890s each Power had a small group of people within its War Office whose duty it was to handle secret information received about other countries. In France this was the misleadingly named Statistical Section, made up of four officers and a filing clerk. As yet very little had been done to make it difficult for spies to collect information. Secret documents were widely distributed and it was hardly noticed if one went missing. It was not difficult to arrange to have a copy made of a document that only existed in its original handwritten form, and so leakages of information were almost certain to happen. It was almost impossible to identify the culprit after the event.

One of the few initiatives that the Statistical Section had taken to gather information for itself was to make an arrangement whereby one of the French servants at the German Embassy in Paris collected together all the contents of the waste-paper baskets and handed them over for inspection. In September 1894 Major Henry, one of the members of the Statistical Section, found an important letter as he searched through the waste paper. It was handwritten and read:

1  Without news indicating that you wish to see me, nevertheless, Sir,
I send you some interesting information:
1. A note on the hydraulic buffer of the 120 and the way in which this gun behaves;
5  2. A note on the covering troops (some modifications will be made under the new plan);
3. A note on a modification to the artillery formations;
4. A note about Madagascar;
5. The preliminary Firing Manual of the Field Artillery (14 March
10  1894).

The last document is extremely difficult to come by and I can
only have it at my disposal for very few days. The War Office has
sent a limited number to the Corps, and the Corps are responsible
for them. Each officer holding one must return it after manoeuvres.
15    If therefore you wish to take from it what interests you and then
keep it for me, I will fetch it. Unless you would like me to have it
copied in extenso and only send you the copy.
I am just off to maneouvres.

Major Henry was delighted. Rumours of a 'leak' had been circulating
for some time and he had been told by his superiors that the spy must be
found quickly because the Minister of War was under attack on other
matters and needed a success with which to fend off his political enemies.
This letter, known throughout the Dreyfus Affair as the *bordereau* (list)
because it contained a list of documents being offered to the Germans,
was unsigned. But it was thought to contain enough internal clues to
allow the culprit to be identified. It was, after all, handwritten.

## a) Dreyfus Convicted

Three conclusions were rapidly reached from a study of the contents of
the *bordereau*. The writer was probably an expert in artillery because of
the nature of documents 1, 3, and 5. He must be a member of the War
Office to have access to such a range of documents. And he was probably
one of the officers recently appointed to the War Office because such
people spent a few months in each section and therefore would have come
across all the documents listed in the *bordereau*. Each member of the War
Office was checked in turn to see whether or not he fitted. When the
name of Captain Alfred Dreyfus was considered it immediately seemed
obvious to Major Henry and his colleagues that here was their man.
Dreyfus was an artillery officer, he was in the process of spending an
amount of time in each section of the War Office, and he seemed the type
of person who was likely to come under suspicion for some malpractice or
another. He was generally unpopular being both arrogant and overkeen.
He was not 'one of the lads'. His zeal in studying the detail of documents
he was shown had already caused some questions to be asked. But most
of all he was suspect in Major Henry's anti-Semitic mind because he was
a Jew. In fact, he was the first Jew ever to be posted to the War Office. It
was known that although he and most of his family had moved into
France from Alsace when it was annexed by Germany in 1871, care had
been taken to leave some brothers behind who could continue to run the
family's factory. This seemed to confirm the widely held prejudice that
Jews were more concerned about financial gain than loyalty to a country.
It was decided that Dreyfus must be the culprit. When some handwriting
experts were prepared to say that the *bordereau* had been penned by
Dreyfus the case seemed solid to Major Henry.

The evidence was laid before Henry's superiors, right up to the
Minister of War himself. As the Minister had already rather unwisely

*Alfred Dreyfus*

declared that the spy was about to be uncovered, he had little choice but to agree that a court martial should be arranged to try Dreyfus on charges of spying. The trial was held in December 1894, and despite passionate denials of guilt by Dreyfus, he was found guilty and sentenced to 'deportation for life to a fortified place'. An especially unpleasant 'fortified place' was chosen for him. It was Devil's Island off the northern coast of South America. This tiny island only 1¼ square kilometres in size was cleared of its occupants, a colony of lepers, so that its sole inhabitants would be Dreyfus and a guard who was forbidden to speak to him. It was confidently expected that fever or madness would soon rid the country of an unwanted prisoner. It appeared that the case was closed. Politicians and newspapers of all persuasions had rejoiced that the traitor had been caught and the government was congratulated on the promptness and effectiveness of its action.

## b) New Evidence

There the matter might have rested had it not been for two factors: the Dreyfus family was convinced of Alfred's innocence and was determined to prove it, and there was appointed to the leadership of the Statistical Section in 1895 a man, Major Picquart, who was scrupulously honest. Between them, although working totally independently, they were able to establish the probability that a great mistake had been made.

The Dreyfus family, because they were not able to gain access to the secret files at the War Office, were forced to pin their hopes of obtaining a retrial on the grounds of some procedural irregularity. Although the bordereau had been paraded at the trial as the major piece of evidence proving Dreyfus' guilt, there was a strong suspicion that the officers who were the judges at the court martial had been shown a secret file of evidence which was claimed to damn the accused absolutely. For such a secret file to be used without making its contents available to the defence was highly improper. Once it became common knowledge that this had in fact happened, the family was able to press to be told what was in the file and to argue that a retrial was necessary. This pressure was resisted by the army authorities who were generally certain of Dreyfus' guilt, although they were aware that the evidence was somewhat thin. They did not want the dubiousness of this evidence to be revealed publicly.

Picquart's position was even more difficult. As a loyal officer of the army and as somebody who had been peripherally involved in identifying Dreyfus as the probable spy, his inclination was to close his mind to the possibility that a mistake had been made. But as an honest man he had to admit to himself that the secret file of evidence which he had been told yielded conclusive proof of Dreyfus' guilt was made up of nothing more than circumstantial evidence of very little worth. His apprehension turned to real concern when it became clear that the German Embassy was still receiving secret documents, and to near panic in 1896 when the

Embassy's waste-paper baskets yielded a letter, presumably thrown away because the writer was not happy with the wording, addressed to a Major Esterhazy in terms which seemed to indicate that he was a spy. Picquart's conscience was troubled almost beyond endurance when Esterhazy's handwriting was shown to be identical with that of the *bordereau*.

Picquart (now a Colonel) entrusted his findings to the army's senior staff and to the Minister of War. They decided that more harm was to be done by correcting the mistake at this stage, when it had been consistently claimed that there was certain proof of Dreyfus' guilt, than by hiding the new evidence and eventually moving Esterhazy to foreign parts where he could do no more damage. Picquart reluctantly accepted this decision. He consoled himself with the notion that Dreyfus and Esterhazy had been partners in crime and set about discovering less circumstantial proof of Esterhazy's guilt.

It was now that events got really out of hand. Major Henry, whose determination to protect the honour of the army was extreme, decided that incontestable evidence of Dreyfus' spying activity must be provided. Because he had no doubt that the end justified the means, he proceeded to forge what was necessary. Pretending that it had come to him in pieces from the German Embassy's waste-paper baskets, he wrote a letter from the Italian military attaché to his German opposite number. It read:

1  I have read that a deputy is going to interpellate [ask questions in parliament] about Dreyfus. If new explanations are needed at Rome, I shall say I have never had relations with this Jew. You understand. If you are asked, say the same thing, for no one must
5  ever know what happened with him.

This forgery, known as the *faux Henry*, was shown to the jubilant army leaders who were now able to say with even greater confidence that there was no possibility that the decision of the court martial had been wrong. At the same time, Henry, who realized that Picquart could not be relied on to remain silent for ever, set about a complicated process of discrediting him in the eyes of his superiors. This involved forging more evidence, and working closely with Esterhazy who was prepared to tell whatever lies he was instructed to as long as he remained safe himself.

## c) The Affair

Until late 1897 the attempts to secure a retrial for Dreyfus were causing no great stir, and it looked as if the efforts of Major Henry and of the most senior generals to prevent a re-opening of the case were being successful. Then, at last, the newspapers began to realize that there was perhaps a scandal to be uncovered and a number of articles appeared casting doubt on various aspects of the army's case. Because it was proving impossible to stop rumours circulating which named Major Esterhazy as the real spy, it was decided that he would have to be court-martialled and found innocent in order to show that there was nothing to hide. At the same time the disgrace of Picquart was completed. He was arrested and subsequently dismissed from the service on grounds of indiscipline.

Suddenly the whole nature of the Dreyfus Affair was changed. What had been a minor matter that rarely surfaced from the privacy of individual conversations and discreet inquiries now became an issue of great public concern that was of importance to the whole of the politically conscious population.

On 13 January 1898 there appeared the most famous open letter of all time, Émile Zola's *'J' Accuse'* ('I accuse'). It was published as the front page of a newspaper and sold several hundred thousand copies. In it Zola, a well-known but not highly respected novelist with a greatly exaggerated opinion of his own importance, accused 'them', the bureaucracy of the Government and the army, of a series of misdemeanors and deceptions spreading from the court martial of Dreyfus to that of Esterhazy. He put into words the misgivings that had been gaining widespread circulation in the previous few months and generalized the issue from the guilt or innocence of one man to questions of the rights of the individual against the all-powerful state and of whether the army was above the law or was subject to it. After a lengthy discussion of the wider issues, Zola made his detailed accusations.

1   I accuse Lieutenant Colonel du Pary de Clam of having been the diabolical worker of the judicial error, I would like to believe unconsciously, and of having afterwards defended his baneful work for three years by the most absurd and culpable
5   machinations.

I accuse General Mercier of having been an accomplice, at least by reasons of weakness of spirit, in one of the greatest iniquities of the century.

I accuse General Billot of having had in his hands certain proofs
10   of the innocence of Dreyfus and of having suppressed them, of having incurred the guilt of this crime of betraying humanity and justice for a political end and to save the compromised General Staff.

I accuse General de Boisdeffre and General Gonse of being
15   accomplices in the same crime, one no doubt from clericalist passion, the other perhaps from that *esprit de corps* which makes the offices of War an unassailable Holy Ark.

I accuse General Pellieux and Major Ravary of having conducted a criminal investigation. I mean by that an investigation of the most
20   monstrous partiality, of which we have, in the latter's report, an imperishable monument of naïve audacity.

I accuse the three handwriting experts, Messrs. Belhomme,

Varinard, and Couard, of having made lying and fraudulent
reports, unless a medical examination finds them stricken by
25 diseased views and judgment.

I accuse the offices of War of having led an abominable press
campaign, especially in *L'Éclair* and in *L'Echo de Paris*, to
mislead opinion and conceal their blame.

I accuse, finally, the first Court-Martial of having broken the law
30 by condemning the accused on secret evidence, and I accuse the
second Court-Martial of having hidden this illegality, on orders,
and of committing in turn the juridical crime of knowingly
acquitting a guilty man . . .

As for the people whom I accuse, I do not know them, I have
35 never seen them, I bear them no bitterness nor hate. For me they
are only entities, spirits of social evil-doing. And the act I am
accomplishing here is only a revolutionary means to hasten the
explosion of truth and justice.

This immediately struck a chord with a large number of educated
Frenchmen of republican sympathies who shared with Zola the fear that
the State, and especially its military arm, was becoming too powerful at
the expense of individual freedoms. Almost overnight, a minor campaign
conducted by a few people to secure justice for a known person became a
major crusade to diminish the power and influence of 'the establishment'
and to re-affirm the principles of liberty, equality and fraternity that lay
at the heart of the style of republicanism that had been popular in France
since 1789. Dreyfus became a symbol. It was almost as if the man and his
continuing suffering had ceased to exist.

The impact of the open letter was quickly followed by a trial in which
the Government responded to Zola's challenge to prosecute him for the
views he had expressed. In the full glare of publicity, with much rhetoric
and many high sounding phrases, the issue was fought. Zola and his
publisher were found guilty of falsely accusing the judges in the Esterhazy trial of acting under government direction and were sentenced to a
period in jail. Zola avoided imprisonment by going to live in England.
The government had theoretically won a victory, but in practice Zola had
achieved all he had hoped for. He had gained a huge amount of publicity
for himself and had helped to raise public consciousness of the dangers
of increased military influence in government circles. But much more
than this had been done.

Politically conscious France had been divided into two camps, the
Dreyfusards and the anti-Dreyfusards, for there were very few people of
any education or social standing who were able to remain neutral. Often
according to previous prejudice or general disposition, each person felt
obliged to be either for Dreyfus or against him. Those who were anti-
Semites, fervent nationalists, in favour of a militarily strong France,
believers in discipline and authority, hostile to a parliamentary

democracy or supporters of the Catholic Church tended to be against Dreyfus. Those who were active Republicans, socialists, pacifists, or anti-clericals tended to be in favour of him. It is said, although without any quantitative evidence being presented, that the Affair (as it was from now on called) divided families, ended long-established friendships and even destroyed business partnerships such was the violence of emotion it generated. For two years the Affair was the main headline news story, and politics seemed to be concerned with little else.

  * In the summer of 1898 the army's case crumbled further. The *faux Henry* was re-examined and was found to be a forgery. Henry, in making it, had stuck together pieces of paper that appeared to be identical but which were actually clearly different when the colouring of the background lines was studied. It was obvious that Henry had reconstructed a sheet of paper from pieces in the German Embassy's waste-paper baskets (most of the documents acquired from this source had been received in little pieces and had then been put together like jigsaws) and had used an original heading and signature but had supplied his own text in between. He confirmed his guilt by taking his razor and cutting his throat. All reasonable people could see that enough doubt had now been cast on the evidence used in the 1894 court martial for Dreyfus to deserve a retrial. The problem was that such entrenched positions had been taken that it was difficult to think of a way of handling matters which would not result in the credibility and morale of the army being totally destroyed.

  As, in late 1898 and early 1899, the Dreyfusards worked through the law courts in an attempt to gain a new trial, feelings were running so high in Paris that a military *coup* to put an end to the Affair was confidently expected or greatly feared, depending on each individual's point of view. The extreme fringe of the anti-Dreyfusard camp, fuelled by the daily invective of Drumont's *Libre Parole*, attempted to bring sufficient violence on to the streets to make an intervention by the army a necessity. They arranged demonstrations but they failed to turn them into full-scale riots for they were poorly led and insufficiently supported. A *coup* was attempted by them on the occasion of the funeral of the President of the Republic, Félix Faure, whose death in the arms of a female friend in very embarrassing circumstances seemed to mark the low point in Republican fortunes, but their organization was pathetically poor and no army commanders could be found to support their efforts.

  Nevertheless, the supporters of the regime were sufficiently concerned about the situation to decide that they must forget their differences and combine together to support a government that would be strong enough to carry the country through what looked like being stormy times ahead. In June 1899 a Government of Republican Defence was formed under Waldeck-Rousseau, one of the most forceful personalities of the Third Republic. His attributes of determination and incisiveness were much needed now, although they were what made him unpopular among fellow politicians in normal times. Waldeck-Rousseau acted decisively

*Dreyfus crucified.*

and wisely. He made it clear to the army that he would protect their honour and ensure that no action was taken against them, but he insisted that the Affair must be settled by Dreyfus being granted a retrial. This took place in September and the Government was at pains to point out that it was putting no pressure on the army officers who were the judges at the new court martial. To the anger of his supporters, Dreyfus was again declared to be guilty, although this time with extenuating circumstances. His sentence was reduced. The army had made its conciliatory gesture. Now it was the turn of the Republicans to do likewise. The new President used his powers to grant Dreyfus a pardon and a bill was passed through parliament extending an amnesty to all those who were accused of committing crimes associated with the Affair. A workable compromise had been devised in a situation where no agreement seemed possible. Good sense had prevailed among the leading politicians and the leading generals and the regime was safe.

  * The policy of forgive and forget was not, however, accepted by a large number of the supporters of the two sides. Those closest to Dreyfus had reluctantly to agree that the pardon must be accepted because there was no chance that Dreyfus' health would cope with a second spell on Devil's Island. But they were determined that he should eventually be declared innocent. Equally, many anti-Dreyfusards were not prepared to forget the way in which their opponents had placed the interests of an individual Jew before the strength and honour of the country, and they were looking for ways in which the power and prestige of the army could be enhanced.

  Even when a court of law actually declared Dreyfus innocent in 1906, having taken two years to decide on a verdict after hearing the evidence, the wounds inflicted by the Affair were not allowed to heal. Certainly until 1914, and for many people until much later, the memory of what had happened soured politics and had an effect on almost every decision made. The crisis, in as far as the future of the regime was concerned, was over by early 1900, but the reverberations have continued, with ever decreasing force, right to the present day. More books have been written on the Affair than on almost any other event in French history, and as new evidence comes to light it still provides widespread interest.

  The most noticeable effect of the Affair was the hardening of the line between those who supported the Republic and those who thought it should be replaced by a different system of government. During the 1880s, and most of the 1890s, despite the temporary setback of Boulangism, many people who had regarded themselves as anti-republicans in the 1870s had accepted that the regime was permanent and that they had better make the most of it. But the Dreyfus Affair drove most of these lukewarm supporters of the Third Republic back into the opposition camp. They did not know what sort of regime they wanted, but they were certain they were not satisfied with what they had. After 1900 there was never any real likelihood that they would engineer a *coup*, but their vocal presence in parliament and in the newspapers kept alive the feeling that France was indeed a divided society.

On the other side of the divide, the effect of the Affair on the Republicans was in many ways beneficial. As Boulangism had done to a lesser extent, the events of 1898 and 1899 brought home to many people the danger of taking the regime for granted. There was a growing realization that more was expected of the Republic than an absence of legislation in favour of the Church and the rich, and that positive steps must be taken to turn into reality many of the vague promises that Republican politicians had been making for many years. Therefore the years after 1900 saw attempts made to further Republican policies through legislative means. It is unlikely that this would have happened had it not been for the spur provided by the Affair.

Yet what has made the events surrounding Alfred Dreyfus of compelling interest to generations of historians and readers of history has been the air of mystery and uncertainty that has even now not been dispelled. Although there are really no grounds for continuing to maintain that Dreyfus was guilty, there is still plenty of room for disagreements about the exact parts played by Henry, Picquart and Esterhazy, and for arguments about how far the anti-Dreyfusards were attempting to undermine the rule of law or how far the Dreyfusards were in effect weakening France's ability to resist the growing German menace. So the debate continues.

---

*Making notes on* 'The Panama Scandal and the Dreyfus Affair'

This chapter falls into two parts. With both the Panama Scandal and the Dreyfus Affair your aim should be the same: to understand what happened and why, and to reach conclusions on what were the effects of the affairs. But because you will probably be asked to write at length about the effects, rather than to give a lengthy account of what happened, it is important that your notes on effects are much fuller than those on the events themselves.

The following headings and sub-headings should help you:

1.    The Panama Scandal
1.1.  Background
1.2.  The Panama Canal Company
1.3.  Causes of collapse
1.4.  The Scandal
1.5.  Effects
2.    The Dreyfus Affair
2.1.  Background
2.2.  Dreyfus convicted
2.3.  New evidence

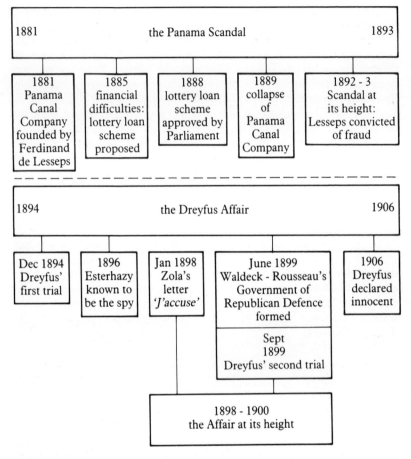

*Summary – The Panama Scandal and the Dreyfus Affair*

2.4. The Affair becomes public
2.5. Dreyfus retried
2.6. Effects

---

**Answering essay questions on *'The Panama Scandal and the Dreyfus Affair'***

Both events discussed in this chapter are likely to feature prominently in general essays on the Third Republic. This is especially so in the case of 'what threats?' questions.

In such essays it is tempting to plan a paragraph on each affair or scandal and to write a narrative rather than an analysis. A way of avoiding this is to make your paragraph points span elements of more than one event. For instance you could approach a 'what threats?' question by drawing up a list of statements such as, 'public confidence in politicians was lowered when it was shown that some of them were corrupt' and 'political divisions were accentuated rather than reduced'.

Think of a number of such statements that could be added to the two examples to provide coverage of a 'what threats?' question. You should have between five and seven statements in total. For each one write a supplementary statement which links it clearly to the question by showing in what way the point you are making posed a threat to the continued existence of the Third Republic. What facts and evidence would you include to support each point?

Occasionally questions appear to be restricted to the Dreyfus Affair alone, but they are normally an invitation to discuss the Affair in the context of the much wider issues involved. A narrative of the Affair, starting in 1894 and ending in 1906, would gain little credit. Two examples of such questions are:

' "In the Dreyfus case, the Third Republic as well as Dreyfus was on trial." Comment on this claim.' (Cambridge, 1982)

'Discuss the significance of the Dreyfus Affair in the history of the Third Republic before 1914.' (Oxford and Cambridge, 1983)

Both examples are variants on the 'what was the significance of . . .' type of question. Two approaches which provide an analytical rather than a narrative structure are:

1. to use the chronological categories of immediate effects short—medium term effects and long term effects, (see page 25);
2. to discuss the impact of the Dreyfus Affair on different aspects of life, such as politics, society, religion and the armed services.

Spend a few minutes planning an answer to the second question using each of these approaches. When you have decided which approach seems most appropriate in this case, plan a detailed answer using it. For each paragraph write an opening sentence which states the point. List the evidence that you will include to support it. Decide on the order in which your paragraphs would appear. What criteria did you use in reaching this decision? (see pages 99 and 100).

---

### Source-based questions on *the Dreyfus Affair*

#### 1 The *bordereau*
Read carefully the *bordereau* and the description of the conclusions

Major Henry reached about it, (pages 71 and 72).
Answer the following questions:
a)   What general types of information was the writer of the *bordereau* offering to the Germans?
b)   What conclusions can be drawn from the *bordereau* about the working relationship between the spy and the recipient of the letter in the German Embassy?
c)   There is evidence in the *bordereau* that Major Henry looked in the wrong place for the spy. What is this evidence? What conclusion does it suggest?

## 2 The *faux Henry*
Read carefully the *faux Henry*, (page 75), and answer the following question:
a)   The *faux Henry* was generally a clever forgery in terms of its content, but one part of it ought not to have rung true to any reader who was prepared to doubt its authenticity. Which part was this? Explain your answer.

## 3 Zola's 'J'accuse'
Read carefully the extract from Zola's letter, given on pages 76 and 77. Answer the following questions:
a)   What is the central issue at stake as far as Zola is concerned?
b)   Although Zola accuses each officer of a specific crime, it is possible to summarize his argument in a general way. Complete the sentence, 'Zola accuses the army of . . .' in less than 20 words.
c)   Zola asserts the motives of three of those he accuses. What are these motives, and which statement about them comes nearest to being a general slur?
d)   Give examples of three phrases where Zola is more interested in effect than in exact meaning.

## 4 Alfred Dreyfus
Study carefully the photograph of Dreyfus reproduced on page 73 and the drawing reproduced on page 79. Answer the following questions:
a)   Estimate the years in which i) the photograph was taken and ii) the drawing was made. Explain your answers fully.
b)   How far does the photograph substantiate the comments made about Dreyfus on page 72?
c)   What seems to be the point of view of the artist who made the drawing? Explain your answer.

# CHAPTER 6

# Issues and Concerns

## 1 Anti-clericalism

Probably the issue that most clearly separated the Left from the Right in the politics of the Third Republic between 1870 and 1914 was the role of the Catholic Church. Ever since 1789 republicanism and anti-clericalism had tended to go hand in hand, while devoted followers of the Church had tended to support forms of government other than a republic. But from 1870, and certainly from 1900, the lines of battle were even more firmly drawn. In particular, ardent Republicans wished for active steps to be taken to reduce the influence of the Church in all aspects of life, but especially in education.

Ferry, in the early 1880s had instigated the first really significant attacks on the Church's position and he had done enough (although the actual changes were in fact not great) to take the heat out of the situation. With the balance of power resting securely in the hands of the more conservative Republicans in the years after 1885, the drive for further legislative action largely disappeared, although it was constantly called for by the politicians of the far Left.

For a time religion ceased to be a major political issue. There was even the possibility that the divide between irreligious Republicans and religious anti-Republicans might disappear when the Pope in the early 1890s gave clear advice to his followers in France to accept and support the Republic. But the *Ralliement*, as this attempt to rally Catholics to the regime was called, was largely a failure. A few prominent Catholic politicians heeded the call but generally the response was poor. The bishops set the tone by treating the new approach as a temporary change in policy that would disappear with the present Pope and the majority of the laity could find no enthusiasm with which to answer the call. The hope of establishing a strong Catholic party within the Republican fold turned out to be a pipe dream.

Yet the easy truce between the two factions seemed set to continue for some time. The Church was allowed to get on with its business without interference and Republican politicians were not subjected to verbal harassment by the clergy. The Dreyfus Affair changed all this. Although many of the Church's leaders in France had enough sense to resist the temptation to make public statements on the issue, much of the leadership for the anti-Dreyfusards was provided by Catholic clergy. Much of what they had to say was highly inflammatory and they were directly responsible for much of the heat that the Affair generated. Their action made it very likely that the Republican politicians would seek their revenge by passing laws aimed at limiting their influence. This became certain once it was clear that the only thing on which the Government's supporters could agree, besides the negative point of preventing the overthrow of the regime, was action against the Catholic Church.

## a) The Attack on the Church

The first target was the religious orders. These were made up of groups of men and women – monks and nuns – who had taken vows of poverty, chastity and obedience in joining one of the orders, most of which were dedicated to 'good works', especially the running of schools and hospitals. The religious orders owned property and received gifts of money which they used to further their work. Nobody had great objections to their work with the sick, although the far Left believed that the State should shoulder these responsibilities, but their educational work had always been contentious. Most Republicans felt that if the religious orders were prevented from indoctrinating the young, the Church would lose its influence within a generation. Ferry had attempted to do this in his education reforms but without complete success.

Following the changed attitudes brought about by the Dreyfus Affair another concerted effort was made during the premiership of Émile Combes from 1902 to 1905. Combes had trained to be a priest before changing his mind. As he matured he developed a great hatred of the Church. He was the most anti-clerical of the Republican politicians and set about the task of destroying the orders with great enthusiasm. Many of them were disbanded but it proved impractical, as it had for Ferry, to ban their ex-members from teaching immediately, for without them the schools could not be staffed. So they were told they would only be allowed to teach for the next ten years, which both gave hope of clerical influence on education eventually ceasing, and allowed time for secular teachers to be trained. But anti-clerical hopes were to be dashed. The coming of the First World War led to an indefinite suspension of this law.

To attack the religious orders was acceptable to all Republicans, but it did not go far enough for many of them. The real aim of the far Left was to end the arrangement between the State and the Pope, first made by Napoleon I, whereby Catholic clergy were paid and Catholic churches were maintained by the Government in return for an amount of influence in clerical appointments. The achievement of this aim was normally frustrated by the moderate Republicans who did not wish to bring about a major confrontation with the Church. But after the Dreyfus Affair most government supporters accepted that the Church's special position must be brought to an end. In 1905 the Separation Law cancelled the previous arrangement. After decades of attempts the anti-clericals had at last achieved their major aim. Now the Church would have to stand on its own feet without official support, although quite generous financial arrangements were made to cover the transitional period following the passing of the new law. Article 11 of the law stipulated that,

1  The ministers of religion who, after the promulgation of the present Law, shall be more than sixty years of age and who shall

have, during at least thirty years, carried out ecclesiastical duties
remunerated by the State, shall receive an annual pension and
5  allowance equivalent to three-quarters of their salary.

Those who shall be more than forty-five years of age and who
shall have, during at least twenty years, carried out ecclesiastical
duties remunerated by the State, shall receive an annual pension
and allowance equal to one-half of their salary.

10  In case of the decease of the holders, these pensions shall be
payable to the value of half of their amount to the benefit of the
widow and orphans, who are minors, left by the deceased, and to
the value of one-quarter to the benefit of his widow without children who are minors. When the orphans attain their majority,
15  the pension shall completely cease.

The ministers of religious bodies at present paid by the State,
who shall not be included in the above provisions, shall receive,
during four years beginning from the abolition of the budget for
religious bodies, an allowance equal to the whole of their salary for
20  the first year, to two-thirds of it for the second, to half for the third
and to a third for the fourth.

In communes of less than 1,000 inhabitants and for ministers of
religious bodies who shall continue to carry out their duties there,
the duration of each of the four periods indicated above shall be
25  doubled.

It was expected that the Church would be greatly weakened in the
process and that Catholic funds would now be used up in providing for
their clergy and their churches, leaving little to be spent on education.
But the effects of the separation of Church and State were not so
dramatic. Gradually it became clear that there were difficulties in recruit-
ing sufficient young men to the ranks of the now poorly paid parish
priesthood, but there was no great reduction in the proportion of children who attended Church schools. A much more obvious effect of the
change was that the Left had lost a cause that had previously helped to
hold it together. From 1905 onwards anti-clericalism was merely a state
of mind: it had exhausted its political programme. Thus no further
official action against the Church was taken. But a legacy was left
whereby most practising Catholics were automatically hostile to the
Republic.

## 2 Socialism

From the very beginning of the Third Republic the supporters of the
regime had seen that it was likely to be threatened from both the Right
and the Left. But in the late 1870s the forces of the Right lost their
opportunity to keep control of events and were henceforth in steady
decline, although they managed to retain the support of a sizeable
minority, especially in the civil service, the army and the Church.

However they no longer posed a genuine threat, except at moments of great crisis, and could generally be attacked with relative impunity, as the anti-clericals found. The Left, in contrast, was a cause of growing concern.

After the horrors of the Commune and the death or exile of all the known leaders of the extreme Left, the moderate Republicans felt confident that a fatal blow had been dealt to the forces of revolutionary extremism. In one respect they were correct because those who wanted to bring about radical social changes had learnt that the age when these could be achieved by an outburst of civic turmoil and the erection of barricades was past. But they were wrong in believing that the last had been heard of the far Left. To some extent they had only themselves to blame for what happened. As their commitment to liberty and equality extended to their enemies as well as their friends, they were unprepared to see ex-Communards languishing in exile for ever. In 1880 they were allowed to return, and many of them were quickly involved again in political activity aimed at furthering the interests of the underprivileged.

However, their progress was slower than might have been expected. They were forced to rebuild from scratch and were hampered by their chronic disunity. A spirit of compromise was alien to most of them as they each fervently believed that their own strategy for bringing about change was the only one that could possibly be successful. They tended to be as hostile to fellow extremists of different persuasions as they were to the protectors of the status quo who were their real enemies. They also had less fertile ground on which to work than had their counterparts in Germany and Britain. There the growth of heavy industry in large units each employing hundreds or thousands of workers had resulted in the emergence of a huge industrial proletariat of the type Marx had seen as being necessary before socialism could triumph over capitalism. In France much of industry remained concentrated in small workshops and although there was a considerable expansion of large-scale production, by 1914 no more than one in ten of the working population was employed in such concerns. The majority of French workers tended to support politicians who called themselves Radicals and who were dedicated to the preservation of individual rights against intervention from the State (not dissimilar to Gladstonian Liberals in Britain). They tended to be suspicious of the representatives of the extreme Left, the various types of socialists who stressed the need for a strong state able to intervene to protect the collective interests of the working classes.

## a) Extra-Parliamentary Action

As the extreme Left grew slowly in the years after 1880 it divided into two main strands. One was made up of those who favoured working by legal means within the existing parliamentary system. The other refused to have any dealings with what they termed 'the bourgeois state', and hoped instead to overthrow it by extra-parliamentary action as a prelude to replacing it by a collectivist state which would infringe individual rights as far as was necessary to ensure the wellbeing of all. Both strands grew steadily in strength, until they were able to play a major part in events in the years after 1905.

The believers in direct action were to experience several false starts. For a while they pinned their faith in General Boulanger and were convinced that their moment of triumph had come in 1889, only to be deserted when success seemed to be within their grasp. For several years in the early 1890s they were seduced by anarchist ideas into believing that the regime could be toppled by carrying out individual acts of violence against its leading members. Notoriety was achieved in 1894 when Sadi Carnot, the fourth President of the Republic, was stabbed to death by one of their members, who for some reason had abandoned the normal anarchist activity of throwing bombs. But anarchism, with its emphasis on destruction rather than construction, had no depth of support in France even among direct action socialists, and when the government took strong action to punish anyone expressing anarchist sympathies the agitation died down as quickly as it had arisen.

From then on the extra-parliamentary socialists pinned their faith on the newly developing trade unions known as *syndicats*. It was only made legal to form *syndicats* in 1884, but they quickly established themselves in the industries of large-scale employment, especially coal-mining, iron and steel, and transport. They even gained a foothold (without legal protection) among government employees such as postal workers and schoolteachers, although they could be expected to make little headway in the areas of the economy where the 'them' and 'us' mentality was largely absent. It, therefore, is not surprising that before 1914 membership of *syndicats* involved no more than one in forty of the population.

The movement to overthrow the state by means of the trade unions, known as revolutionary syndicalism, was at its height between 1905 and 1908. The views of the Syndicalists were well illustrated by a charter they issued at their annual congress in 1906.

1   In the process of making its everyday demands syndicalism seeks to coordinate the efforts of the workers, to better their conditions through achieving such immediate improvements as shorter working hours, wage increases, etc.
5     But this activity is only one side of the work of syndicalism. It is preparing that complete emancipation, which can be accomplished only when the capitalist is expropriated; it commends the general strike as a means of action, and it believes that the *syndicat*, which is now the nucleus of resistance, will in future become the nucleus
10 for production and distribution, the foundation of social reorganization.

The Congress declares that this double task of everday life and of the future is the outcome of the conditions of wage earners which is burdensome to all workers and makes it the duty of the wage-
15 earning class, whatever their political or philosophical inclinations, to belong to that essential group, the *syndicat*;

Accordingly, so far as individuals are concerned, the Congress declares that all members have complete freedom to take part outside the corporate group in any form of struggle which their
20 political or philosophical beliefs may require, and it confines itself to asking them, in return, not to introduce into the *syndicat* opinions which they profess outside;

So far as organizations are concerned, the Congress decides that, for syndicalism to attain maximum effectiveness, economic action
25 should be exercised directly against the employer class, and the Confederal Organizations must not, as syndicalist groups, pay heed to the parties and sects which, outside and by their sides, are completely free to pursue their aims of social transformation.

The weapon it aimed to use was the general strike, which, it was argued, would bring the country to a standstill and would force the government to hand over its powers. But it proved beyond the capabilities of the syndicalist leaders to organize an effective general strike. They tried to capitalize on various bitter and violent strikes, especially by the miners, to call out other workers but they found (as others have found in many countries since) that they were unable to win the support of people who only hazily understood their ideas and who were unprepared to suffer a loss of income and the possible loss of job in pursuit of an end that would be of no direct benefit to them. Yet the individual strikes themselves were sufficiently widespread, involving much destruction of property and some loss of life, to create an atmosphere of crisis in the country in which it was possible to believe that a revolution was about to break out. Had it not been for the resolute stand made by the Government, the revolutionary syndicalists might have been able to achieve their aims even though they were unable to mobilize the full extent of their support.

## b) Clemenceau

For years when syndicalism was at its height the Prime Minister was Georges Clemenceau, a Radical. Only twice in a political career that spanned more than half a century was he to attain highest office. Once was during his ministry of 1906–9, but his finest hour was to come in the closing stages of the First World War and at the peace conference that followed when, as his country's leader, his stubborn determination to secure victory and to enjoy its fruits earned him the nickname of 'the Tiger'. But when he became Prime Minister for the second time in 1917 he was already 76 years old and was past his best, although he was still a daunting figure. During his prime he had been one of the most feared politicians in the land. It was said that he was equally dangerous with his tongue, his pen and his sword. Although he was a fine duellist, which made opponents very cautious about casting doubt on his honour, it was through his speeches in the Chamber of Deputies and his newspaper articles that he made his greatest mark. These also made him so many enemies that he was only called to power when a crisis was brewing. It was known that he could be relied on to take definite and determined action.

In 1893 when he had been hounded from politics because of his close connection with Cornelius Herz, one of the villains of the Panama Scandal, it appeared that his career had been a failure. He had been regarded as a leader of the radical republicans ever since he had disassociated himself from the Paris Commune at its inception, although he was at the time the Mayor of one of the capital's working class *arrondissements*. But during his whole time as a deputy he had held no political office. Instead, he had built a reputation as the scourge of governments and, with what appeared to be malicious pride, he would claim to be largely responsible for the fall of many of the ministries whose brief lives had added to the instability of the regime. None of the policies he believed in had been implemented: he had no solid achievements to his credit.

The Dreyfus Affair provided Clemenceau with an opportunity to make amends for the past. As one of the leading Dreyfusards – he thought up the title '*J'accuse*' for Zola's open letter – he could take much of the credit for the success of the cause, and was able to gain election to the Senate in 1902 largely as a result of it. He was thus available to hold office, first as Minister of the Interior (the equivalent of the Home Secretary in Britain) and then as Prime Minister during the difficult time of the syndicalists' attempts to overthrow the regime. His attitude towards the trade unionists was very clear. He was able to communicate to them a genuine sympathy for their economic and social grievances, but he was totally unprepared to accept their violence. He was prepared to meet with them and to discuss their problems, but once the talking turned to action he was quick to use the police and the army to restore order, even if lives were lost in the process. Clemenceau's clear determination that law and order should be maintained played a large part in persuading the syndicalists that they would not be successful. By the time he fell from power the crises was over although the strike movement was to continue for a year or more longer.

## c) Parliamentary Action

The socialists who relied on direct action were playing for high stakes. It was a matter of all or nothing. They were not prepared to accept half measures, which they regarded as reinforcing the basic status quo. In contrast, the socialists who were prepared to operate within the existing system appreared to make substantial progress. In each of the general elections from 1893 onwards they secured enough votes to win a steadily increasing number of seats, starting with nearly fifty and ending with over a hundred (exact figures are impossible to give because the dividing line between socialists and radicals was not finely drawn). From 1905 onwards some of their leaders were given ministerial office, although this led to bitter divisions between those who were prepared to co-operate with non-socialists and those, like Jean Jaurès the leading socialist of the time, who were only prepared to become ministers in a purely socialist government. When the legislation of the period is examined it is obvious that the socialists were not able to secure the implementation of any of their basic policies involving a redistribution of wealth and the establishment of a system of social security. The nearest they came to success was over the possible introduction of a system of progressive income tax, in which the rich would pay increasingly more than the poor, but although they were able to fight this through the Chamber of Deputies, it disappeared without trace in the Senate. Despite all the socialists' efforts both inside and outside parliament, the France that entered the World War in August 1914 was not fundamentally different, either economically or socially, from the country that had suffered defeat at the hands of the Prussians 43 years earlier.

## 3 Foreign Affairs

The spectre of German power loomed large in the background of French politics throughout the life of the Third Republic. It rarely forced its way to the foreground of events and only occupied the centre of the stage on a very few occasions, but its influence was regularly felt. It hung like a dark cloud over most of France. It was made up in part of the memory of the disastrous defeat of 1870–71 and the loss of Alsace–Lorraine, and in part of the fear that the same thing might happen again at some time in the future. In all aspects of French foreign policy in the years 1870–1914 there was an ever present German factor.

The vast majority of the French hoped in their heart of hearts that one day they would be able to take their revenge on Germany and win back the lost provinces of Alsace and Lorraine, but it was only the Right that made it a central part of their political programme. Most Republicans were realistic enough to accept that it would probably never happen, and sensed that too much belligerent talk in Paris might encourage the Gemans to carry out a pre-emptive strike. It was Boulanger's posturing towards Germany when he was Minister of War that first alerted his colleagues to the danger he posed, although, of course, it was just this behaviour that endeared him to so many ordinary people. Luckily for their country, most French politicians realized that they had to be cautious in their dealings with Berlin, and were careful not to antagonize their powerful neighbour too much in the pursuit of easy popularity.

France was very slow to recover in diplomatic terms from the shattering blow of the war of 1870–71. It was as if the French needed time to readjust to the fact that they were no longer the dominant Power in Europe. For too long French politicians had been able to afford the luxury of giving offence to each of the other Powers individually, knowing that it would require the unlikely combination of them all to impose their will on France. Suddenly the situation had changed, and the reality was that the French needed friends and allies if they were to be safe from attack, let alone play a major part in international relations.

It was the Right that first accepted the logic of the situation and argued that if the main aim of French foreign policy was to regain Alsace and Lorraine, everything reasonably possible must be done to win the friendship of the European Powers other than Germany. Certainly, they contended, nothing must be done to antagonize them. But by the time they came to this conclusion in the 1880s they had lost power and were doomed to perpetual opposition, sometimes combining with others to bring down the government, but never strong enough to form a ministry of their own.

The Republicans, before 1900, were not committed to seeking a reversal of the verdict of the Franco–Prussian War. But they were united in little else. Although they generally favoured a passive foreign policy, with no risks taken and little expenditure incurred, they showed no common view of the part their country should play in world affairs. This lack of clear purpose resulted in a stumbling and fumbling approach with seemingly contradictory aims being worked towards by successive governments, and on occasion even by different ministers within the same government. Only when Jules Ferry was at his most influential, between 1880 and 1885, was there any consistency of policy over a period of years. His decision to seek greatness for France outside Europe, because this was acceptable to Germany, could be argued to have distracted the country from its true interests. While the growth in the number and extent of French colonies added to her international standing, it brought diplomatic conflict with Britain, and to a lesser extent with Italy, and continued the isolation that made her particularly vulnerable to pressure from Germany.

## a) The Franco–Russian Alliance

When Bismarck fell from power in Berlin in 1890 he had enjoyed 20 years of diplomatic supremacy in Europe. In this he had been helped to no small extent by the muddle-headed and indecisive policies of the French, who only had themselves to blame, rather than the machinations of the German Chancellor, for the fact that they remained friendless in Europe. It has often been claimed that the Franco–Russian Alliance that was announced in 1894 was a direct result of the change of German policy following Bismarck's fall, when the Kaiser made it clear that he regarded

Austria-Hungary rather than Russia as his major ally. This is only a partial truth, because France and Russia had been tottering towards friendship for some time. With hindsight this can be seen to have been a natural partnership for both countries were apprehensive about Germany's intentions, and their geographic positions, one on either side of their potential enemy, meant that they could make Germany divide her forces in time of war. But in the late twentieth century when a country's system of government tends to dictate its international friends and enemies, it may seem odd that the most autocratic and the most democratic of the European Powers should form a friendship. Yet at the time it caused hardly a stir because there was no conception of international relations being a struggle between rival blocs with antagonistic political ideologies. What mattered to most French people, who were generally enthusiastic about the alliance, was that Russia was led by a Francophile upper class that spoke French, wrote in French and enjoyed all things artistically and culturally French. Flattered by this extensive imitation, French people could overlook the fact that the Tsar was the enemy of liberty in his own domains. So there was little but joy expressed when it was announced that by their defensive alliance France and Russia had agreed to come to each other's assistance if either were to be attacked by Germany.

Yet the Franco–Russian Alliance of 1894 should not be seen as marking the emergence of a clear sense of direction in French foreign policy. It was not that the alliance happened totally by chance; more that it grew almost naturally from the situation that existed in Europe and from the good relations that had grown up between the two countries as more and more French capital had been invested in the development of Russia (especially her railways) in the 1880s. Certainly there was no thought on the part of Republican politicians that they were in the process of building up a grouping of states that would one day be able to put a stop to the steady increase of German power. If there had been, successive governments would not have maintained an attitude of hostility towards Britain over colonial matters. This was to bring the two countries to the brink of war in 1898 in the Fashoda Incident in which competing claims for control of the Sudan came to a head. As late as 1900 in Britain, although the country was still in 'splendid isolation', most people looked upon Germany as the natural friend and France as the natural enemy.

## b) The Anglo–French Entente

Within a few years all this had changed. The British government came to understand that Germany meant to challenge seriously for supremacy of the seas. French politicians, operating in the heightened atmosphere of reality that followed the Dreyfus Affair, came to the conclusion that it made more sense to give way to Britain on numbers of colonial issues in order to win her support in dealings with Germany than to maintain the bitter rivalry. So, much against the trend of recent events, the Anglo–French Entente was formed in 1904. Because Britain was not yet ready to abandon her isolation in Europe (an alliance with Japan had been signed in 1902) the Entente was in writing no more than a settlement of colonial disputes, but in practice its underlying assumption was that in time of European war the two countries would find themselves on the same side. There were many doubts and misunderstandings as the two countries made efforts to co-ordinate their military preparations during the following decade, but most of these came from the British side where there was great nervousness about doing anything that might be read as a definite commitment. As far as France was concerned a choice had been made. It was not only that Russia and Britain were to be cultivated as friends: it was also that Germany would be stood up to, even if the end result was to be a war forced on her by German intransigence. This new determination was a marked feature of most governments from 1899 onwards and became as much of a consistent policy as was possible in a situation of rapidly changing ministries. So, German attempts to score diplomatic victories in the two Moroccan crises of 1905–6 and 1911 were stoutly resisted. With a modicum of support from Britain and Russia, France was successful in obtaining agreements that were to her advantage in that she was able to take control of Morocco, thus extending her north African empire, without paying too high a price to Germany as 'compensation'.

The Kaiser seems to have come to the conclusion that the series of agreements France had made with Russia and Britain had resulted in the formation of a powerful anti-German bloc. He believed that Germany would only be able to have as much influence in the world as her size and strength warranted if the grouping that had been formed against her was smashed. Thus, in 1914, advantage was taken of the assassination of the heir to the Austro–Hungarian crowns to manufacture a crisis as a result of which Russia and France would be attacked whatever they did. The Germans assumed that Britain would have enough sense to stay out of a war that did not really concern them. In August, therefore, what most French people had known would happen at some time took place: Germany attempted to invade France once again. But France was quite well prepared. She had friends upon whom she could rely. Her armed forces were soundly organized and equipped, with morale that had recovered from the blows of the Dreyfus Affair. But most of all, she had leading politicians who were able to stand resolute when the great crisis came.

The Third Republic might have survived so long because it was the form of government that divided French people least, but it also had the positive merit of being able to respond to major challenges as they came. This no other regime since the Revolution had been able to do.

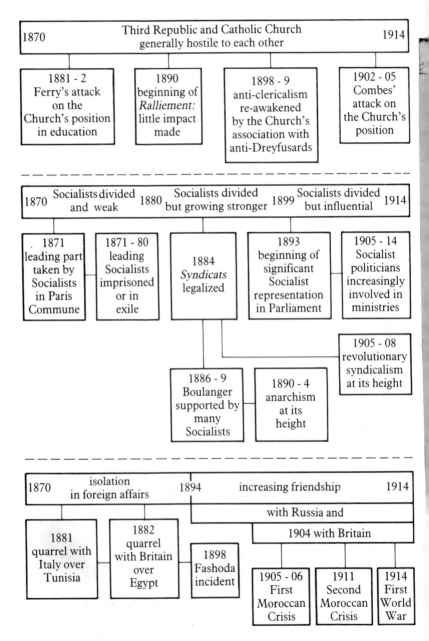

| 1870 | Third Republic and Catholic Church generally hostile to each other | | 1914 |

| 1881 - 2 Ferry's attack on the Church's position in education | 1890 beginning of *Ralliement:* little impact made | 1898 - 9 anti-clericalism re-awakened by the Church's association with anti-Dreyfusards | 1902 - 05 Combes' attack on the Church's position |

| 1870 | Socialists divided and weak | 1880 | Socialists divided but growing stronger | 1899 | Socialists divided but influential | 1914 |

| 1871 leading part taken by Socialists in Paris Commune | 1871 - 80 leading Socialists imprisoned or in exile | 1884 *Syndicats* legalized | 1893 beginning of significant Socialist representation in Parliament | 1905 - 14 Socialist politicians increasingly involved in ministries |

| 1905 - 08 revolutionary syndicalism at its height |

| 1886 - 9 Boulanger supported by many Socialists | 1890 - 4 anarchism at its height |

| 1870 | isolation in foreign affairs | 1894 | increasing friendship | 1914 |

with Russia and

1904 with Britain

| 1881 quarrel with Italy over Tunisia | 1882 quarrel with Britain over Egypt | 1898 Fashoda incident | 1905 - 06 First Moroccan Crisis | 1911 Second Moroccan Crisis | 1914 First World War |

*Summary – Issues and Concerns*

*Making notes on 'Issues and Concerns'*

The three topics dealt with in this chapter highlight the issues that were of most concern to politically-minded French people in the years after 1900. The notes you make should help to remind you why each of the issues was thought to be important; what was done; and with what effects.
The following headings and sub-headings should assist you:

1.   Anti-clericalism
1.1. Background (to 1900)
1.2. The attack on the Church (1902–5)
2.   Socialism
2.1. Background
2.2. Extra-parliamentary action
2.3. Clemenceau
2.4. Parliamentary action
3.   Foreign affairs
3.1. Background
3.2. The Franco–Russian Alliance (1894)
3.3. The Anglo–French Entente (1904)

---

*Answering essay questions on 'Issues and Concerns'*

There is a tendency to think of the period from about 1899 to 1914 as quite distinct from the preceding 30 years. This is shown both by the fact that general questions often specify the end of the century as their closing date, and by the fact that specific questions about the years immediately preceding 1914 sometimes appear.
Three examples of the latter are:

' "Between 1899 and 1914 clericalism and socialism were the main targets of French Republican governments." How successfully did they deal with them?' (Oxford)
'Did the Third French Republic achieve political and social stability in the twenty years before 1914?' (Oxford)
' "The apparent weakness displayed by France in the period 1894–1914 resulted from the dominance of a single issue, the Dreyfus Affair." How valid is this statement?' (JMB)

All these questions require answers that consider differing points of view. In each case a two-part essay should be planned. One half gives the answer, 'Yes, in these ways/to this extent . . .'. The other half argues, 'No, not in these ways/to this extent . . . .'.

If you are used to answering this type of question you will be able to plan your answer directly by listing the paragraph points you would wish to include in each half. But if your experience of such questions is limited, you might find it helpful to list all the facts/evidence you have that is relevant to the essay title in question.

Once you have your list, attempt to link facts/evidence together to make a general point. Then assign it to either the 'Yes' or the 'No' halves of your plan.

For example, if you employ this strategy with the first of the three essay titles, you will find it possible to make general points about the attack on the Church's control of education, and the lessening support of the Church by the State. Both of these general points will need to be covered in both halves of the essay. What other general points could you make? List them, along with the facts/evidence to support them.

A similar approach could be adopted with a question such as,

' "The Tiger'. Was this nickname for Clemenceau justified in his political career before 1914?' (Cambridge)

Re-read the sub-section on Clemenceau (pp 90–1) and note down the facts/evidence that could be used in answering this question. Group them together to make general points. Assign them to either or both of 'Yes, it was justified' and 'No, it was not justified'. When you have studied pp 99–100, decide what order you would use in presenting your points.

---

***Source-based questions on** 'Issues and Concerns'*
**1 Separation Law, 1905**
Read carefully the extract from the Separation Law, given on pages 86 and 87. Answer the following questions:

a) Was this section of the Separation Law likely to have been supported by those who most strongly championed the cause of separation of church and state? Give full reasons for your answer.
b) What are the implications of the final paragraph of the extract, (lines 22–5)?

**2 Syndicalist Charter, 1906**
Read carefully the extract from the Syndicalist Charter, given on pages 89 and 90. Answer the following questions:

a) What evidence does the Charter provide about the long-term aims of the Syndicalists?
b) What evidence does the Charter provide about the methods of the Syndicalists?
c) What conclusions about the degree of unity among the Syndicalists can be drawn from the penultimate paragraph, (lines 17–22), of the extract?

*Answering essay questions on France 1870–1914*

On page 6 you will find six examples of typical questions on the general topic of France 1870–1914. Now is the time to look at them again and to note down for each one the factors/issues that will provide you with your paragraph headings.

Pay particular attention to the exact wording of the questions as you make your decisions. For instance, the Oxford question on 'what threats' has a finishing date of 1895. This means that no credit would be given for a discussion of the Dreyfus Affair, which did not become a matter of widespread public concern until after 1895. Once you have decided on your paragraph headings and have checked that they fall within the scope of the wording of the question, you need to arrange them in the most appropriate order to provide a convincing answer.

Sometimes it appears sensible to deal with your points in chronological order. But this is dangerous. If you are not careful you will rapidly fall into the trap of writing a narrative essay rather than an analytical one which includes carefully selected narrative and evidence to support an argument you are putting forward. It is better to look for a method of grouping or ordering your points that does not depend on chronology.

Two obvious approaches are based on the relative significance of the points you wish to make. You could start with the most important and go on to the other factors in descending order of significance. Or you could begin with the minor issues and build up to your major point. Either approach can provide the framework for an effective answer.

Equally, you could group your points according to the broad aspect of history to which they belong, such as political, social, economic or religious. If you adopt this approach, which is often the best way of ensuring that general analytical points are made, you must include a final paragraph that comments on the relative significance of the points you have made.

To test out the four ways of grouping/ordering paragraph points as described above (chronological; from most to least important; from least to most important; by broad aspects), you might try making four essay plans for the following question:

'How dangerous to the French Third Republic were the chief sources of internal opposition in the period 1871–1914?' (AEB, 1981)

Decide which plan best answers the question, Why?

Sometimes you will be faced with a question that draws attention (usually in a quote) to one factor/issue, and that asks you to discuss its relative significance. Two examples of such questions are:

' "It is the Republic which divides us least." Was this the reason why the Third Republic survived in 1890?' (Oxford, 1981)

' "The Third Republic in France survived only because every alternative was discredited." Discuss with reference to 1870–1914.' (Oxford and Cambridge, 1982)

The stages to be gone through in preparing to answer such 'challenging statement' types of question are similar irrespective of the topic concerned. The first step is to identify the general topic/issue being asked about. In the examples above this is 'why did the Third Republic survive?' The second step is to identify the factor/issue that is included in the question. In the examples this is the lack of an alternative regime that could attract more support. Thirdly, a list is made of all the other factors that are relevant to the issue. In the examples these would be factors such as the moderation of the Republicans who were in power and the destruction of the revolutionary Left during the Commune.

Lastly an essay plan is drawn up. In this a short introductory paragraph indicates the argument that is to be followed. In 'challenging statement' essays this is preferably *either* 'the factor/answer included in the question was of greater importance, but there are other significant factors/answers such as . . .', *or* 'the factor/answer included in the question is significant but the factors/answers of greatest importance are . . .'.

Then follow paragraphs for each of the factors/answers, starting with the one included in the question. The other paragraphs are placed in order according to one of the four approaches described earlier in this section.

If the essay has been well planned the conclusion need only be brief, drawing attention to the general argument followed and finishing with a sentence that leaves the reader with something to think about, possibly a connection with another historical topic that would not immediately spring to mind. For the first example it might be a sentence such as, 'so the Third Republic survived for the same major reason as the joint allied control of Berlin since 1945: no agreement could be found on a better way of arranging matters.'

You might find it helpful now to draw up an essay plan for the second example, and then write in full the introductory and concluding paragraphs.

When revising this topic it would be sensible to plan and write answers to at least one of the following questions which cover both of the major issues on which this volume concentrates:

> 'What elements in French society were hostile to the Third Republic before 1914, and why were they unable to overthrow it?' (London, 1978)

> 'Assess the strengths and weaknesses of the Third Republic in France before 1914.' (Oxford and Cambridge, 1979)

> 'What domestic problems faced the Third French Republic between 1880 and 1914? How successfully did it cope with them?' (JMB, 1979)

> 'Describe the problems facing the Third French Republic and assess its success in overcoming them.' (Scottish, 1982)

# Further Reading

There are three books, in particular, that could be read in part at least if you are interested in gaining further understanding of the period. They are all quite old and are most appropriate for undergraduates at university, but they are generally well-written, with considerable insight. You would certainly benefit from reading each of them for an hour or so to gain an appreciation of their style. Make no notes while you are reading them, and only very brief ones once you have finished the section(s) you have selected. The three books are:

**Alfred Cobban,** *A History of Modern France, volume 2: 1799–1945,* (Penguin, 1961) – probably best on the 1870s;
**J.P.T. Bury,** *France 1814–1940,* (Methuen, 4th ed 1969) – worth reading chapter XIII; and
**D.W. Brogan,** *The Development of Modern France (1870–1939),* (Hamish Hamilton, 1940) – deals in detail with most political events.

The most readable historian to write in English on the France of this period is Guy Chapman. His books are more detailed than those listed above but are not heavy. In fact they read like novels at times. If you like history you will almost certainly enjoy reading the whole of:

**Guy Chapman,** *The Third Republic of France: The First Phase, 1871–1894,* (MacMillan, 1962) – made up of 23 short chapters that largely stand on their own; and
**Guy Chapman,** *The Dreyfus Trials,* (Batsford, 1972) – like a detective novel.

Four further books would repay a short time spent on them. But they contain much more information than you could possibly require at this level so beware of becoming bogged down in them. The books are:

**Michael Howard,** *The Franco–Prussian War,* (Hart–Davis, 1968);
**Stewart Edwards,** *The Paris Commune 1871,* (Eyre & Spottiswoode, 1971);
**David Robin Watson,** *Georges Clemenceau,* (Eyre Methuen, 1974); and
**Roger Magraw,** *France 1815–1914: The Bourgeois Century,* (Fontana, 1983) – see especially pp 285–317 on Socialism.

One excellent way of revising the whole topic would be to read chapter one (pp 5–29) of **R.D. Anderson,** *France 1870–1914,* (Routledge and Kegan Paul, 1977) which gives a clear overview of the period, although it assumes considerable prior knowledge on the part of the reader.

# Sources on France: The Third Republic, 1870–1914

Relatively little documentary evidence on France during this period is readily available in English.

The most useful general collection of items is to be found in:
1. **David Thomson**, *France: Empire and Republic, 1850–1940* (Macmillan 1968)

The writings of Karl Marx on the Paris Commune can be found in:
2. **Marx and Engels**, *Selected Works*, vol I (Moscow 1951)

or in many of the other selections from their writings which have been published in English.

Little primary source material on the politics of the period is included in secondary works written in or translated into English.
3. **Guy Chapman**, *The Dreyfus Trials* (Batsford 1972) contains both pictorial and documentary evidence, and
4. **Stewart Edwards**, *The Paris Commune 1871* (Eyre & Spottiswoode 1971) has a number of interesting contemporary illustrations.

A range of illustrations on nineteenth-century European history in general is included in:
5. ed. **Asa Briggs**, *The Nineteenth Century* (Thames & Hudson 1970)

## Acknowledgements

Acknowledgement is given for the use of extracts from the above publications as follows:

**David Thomson**, *France: Empire and Republic, 1859–1940* (original French sources are given in brackets) pages 11–12 (*Documents diplomatiques Français*, 1er série, vol 1, Paris 1929; pages 16–17 (*Enquête parlementaire sur l'insurrection du 18 mars*, vol IX, Paris 1872); pages 28–29 (**comte de Falloux**, *Mémoires d'un royaliste*, vol III, Paris 1925); pages 40–41 (**Halévy and Pillias**, *Lettres de Gambetta*, letter 309, Paris 1938); pages 41–42 (**Charles de Freycinet**, *Souvenirs, 1848–1878*, Paris 1912); pages 52–54 (**Paul Robiquet**, *Discours et opinions de Jules Ferry*, vol V, Paris 1897); pages 61–62 (**Charles Chincholle**, *Le Général Boulanger*, Paris 1889).

**Marx and Engels**, *Selected Works* pages 17–18.

**Guy Chapman**, *The Dreyfus Affair* pages 71–72, 79.

The Author and Publishers wish to thank the following for their permission to use copyright illustrations:

The Illustrated London News Picture Library; Cover (the announcement of the election of Casimir-Perier to the Presidency of the Republic, 1894); Bibliothèque Nationale, Paris: p. 20; Bulloz: p. 57; Roger-Viollet: pp. 73, 79.

The Author and Publishers wish to thank the following examination boards for permission to include questions:
The Associated Examining Board; Joint Matriculation Board; Oxford and Cambridge Schools Examination Board; Southern Universities' Joint Board; University of Cambridge Local Examinations Syndicate; University of London School Examinations Department; University of Oxford Delegacy of Local Examinations; Welsh Joint Education Committee; Scottish Certificate of Education Examination Board. (The essay guidance sections are the responsibility of the General Editor and have not been approved by the Boards.)

# Index